FOUNDATIONS OF MODERN ECONOMICS SERIES

Otto Eckstein, *Editor*

UBLISHED

RICHARD B. FREEMAN   *University of Chicago*

Labor Economics

PRENTICE-HALL, INC.   *Englewood Cliffs, New Jersey*

To JTD

ISBN: P 0–13–517458–9

     C 0–13–517466–x

Library of Congress Catalog Number 73–181299

PRENTICE-HALL FOUNDATIONS
OF MODERN ECONOMICS SERIES

Otto Eckstein, *Editor*

10 9 8 7 6 5 4 3 2 1

PRENTICE-HALL INTERNATIONAL INC., *London*
PRENTICE-HALL OF AUSTRALIA, PTY., LTD., *Sydney*
PRENTICE-HALL OF CANADA, LTD., *Toronto*
PRENTLCE-HALL OF INDIA PVT. LIMITED, *New Delhi*
PRENTICE-HALL OF JAPAN, INC., *Tokyo*

Foundations

of Modern Economics Series

Economics has grown so rapidly in recent years, it has increased so much in scope and depth, and the new dominance of the empirical approach has so transformed its character, that no one book can do it justice today. To fill this need, the Foundations of Modern Economics Series was conceived. The Series, brief books written by leading specialists, reflects the structure, content, and key scientific and policy issues of each field. Used in combination, the Series provides the material for the basic one-year college course. The analytical core of economics is presented in *Prices and Markets* and *National Income Analysis*, which are basic to the various fields of application. Two books in the Series, *The Evolution of Modern Economics* and *Economic Development: Past and Present*, can be read without prerequisite and can serve as an introduction to the subject.

The Foundations approach enables an instructor to devise his own course curriculum rather than to follow the format of the traditional textbook. Once analytical principles have been mastered, many sequences of topics can be arranged and specific areas can be explored at length. An instructor not interested in a complete survey course can omit some books and concentrate on a detailed study of a few fields. One-semester courses stressing either macro- or micro-economics can be readily devised. The Instructors Guide to the Series indicates the variety of ways the books in the Series can be used.

The books in the Series are also being used as supplements to the basic textbooks, to permit a fuller curriculum on some topics. Intermediate level courses are using volumes in the Series as the core text and are combining these with various readings.

This Series is an experiment in teaching. The positive response to the first two editions has encouraged us to continue to develop and improve the approach. New books are being added and the previous books revised and updated. The thoughtful reactions of many teachers who have used the books in the past have been of immense help in preparing the third edition.

The books do not offer settled conclusions. They introduce the central problems of each field and indicate how economic analysis enables the reader to think more intelligently about them, to make him a more thoughtful citizen, and to encourage him to pursue the subject further.

Otto Eckstein, *Editor*

Contents

Labor and Society

Hoboes and the idle rich notwithstanding, work is a primary activity for mankind. Every society—feudal, free-enterprise, or collectivist—organizes labor to produce goods and services. It somehow decides what tasks will be performed, who will perform them, and under what rules. It also determines how conflicts arising from these decisions should be resolved. Four major issues constitute the general labor problems of every society.

Wages. What determines wages and changes in wages, in the economy as a whole and in particular sectors, enterprises, and occupations? Why are workers such as construction craftsmen, professional football players, and university professors paid more than laborers or hospital attendants? What is the effect of union or government policies on wage determination?

Employment and job skills. The number of persons employed in certain occupations—mathematicians, airline mechanics, and computer programmers, for example—has increased greatly, whereas the number in other jobs, such as granite cutters, coal miners, and farm laborers has declined. What explains this relative reallocation of employment? How do workers obtain the job skills needed for diverse forms of work? Why do workers move from one locality or occupation to another?

Unemployment. What explains the existence of unemployed workers? Why are nonwhites, unskilled persons, and teenagers more likely to be unemployed than other workers? Is full employment compatible with other economic goals such as price stability, growth in productivity, and industrial peace?

1

Industrial conflict. In what ways are labor–management disputes resolved? What is the role of government in settling disputes? Should public employees, schoolteachers, firemen, and policemen have the same right to organize and strike that private employees have?

More detailed questions arise in setting the rules of every work place and in their day-to-day administration. For example, consider the following issues as representative of contemporary labor problems in the United States:

For years an airline company terminates the employment of stewardesses at age 32. The management regards the rule as sound business judgment and in accord with the preferences of the flying public. A number of stewardesses oppose the rule and seek to have it changed. They argue that their employment opportunities are unreasonably restricted, that experience should be rewarded rather than penalized, and that the traveling public has no prejudices against stewardesses over 32.

An employee of long service argues with his foreman about the quality of his work and is discharged on the spot. The foreman believes that discipline must be maintained and insubordination punished to preserve managerial authority. The employee feels that the foreman is picking on him, that his work is of high quality, and that other employees have not been punished as harshly for similar conduct.

For years a high-wage company has been hiring workers by "word of mouth." Employees, who are predominantly white, tell their friends and relatives about job opportunities, whereas nonwhites rarely learn about them. The NAACP and the federal government argue that the company has an obligation to publicize jobs among nonwhite Americans. The company and current employees disagree with this view.

The wage for a particular job—say, a soaking-pit craneman in a steel plant—must be determined. Management, union officials, and workers compare the job with other jobs in the plant and in other companies, raising issues of comparative skill, responsibility, working conditions, hazards, and educational requirements. The cranemen, like many employees, believe that their wages should be raised above those of other workers. Management notes that its chief competitor pays a lower wage for cranemen. The union is troubled by the relation between the wage for cranemen and that for pitmen who work in the same department.

Similar examples of labor problems arise, albeit in somewhat different forms, in societies with varying political and economic organizations. They are not peculiar to capitalism, private enterprise, or collective bargaining. The nationalized industries of Western Europe, plants under workers' management in Yugoslavia, and the state enterprises of the Soviet Union all face issues of determining wages, establishing work rules, and allocating jobs. Particular aspects of problems may be associated with different kinds of economic organization, but comparable issues are common to all industrial economies.

TOOLS OF ANALYSIS

Several analytic tools are useful in understanding labor problems. One set of tools is offered by the economic theory of markets; a second set, concerned with the major institutions in the labor market, is found in the study of industrial relations. An entirely different perspective is provided by the theories associated with Karl Marx.

Market Analysis: Price Theory

The market approach deals primarily with the determination of wages and employment, and ordinarily treats other phenomena, such as work rules relating to safety or promotion, as given or inconsequential for the problems under study. The market is depicted by supply-and-demand schedules which represent the response of individuals and employers to economic incentive. The intersection of supply and demand determines the *equilibrium* wage and employment in a particular market (Fig. 1–1).

Although markets may never in fact attain equilibrium, analysis of equilibrium is useful in understanding developments because variables such as wages or employment normally move toward equilibrium over time. Knowledge of equi-

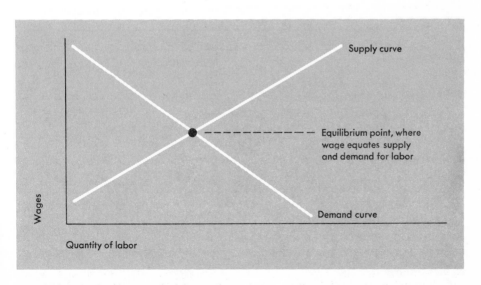

FIG. 1–1   Equilibrium in the labor market.

librium wages or employment can help predict the general direction of change when a market is in disequilibrium or when its equilibrium changes because of new circumstances. Supplemented with information about the *process of adjustment*, especially of the time required for employers or individuals to react to new conditions, the market approach offers many insights into behavior.

Labor markets differ greatly in their economic and social organization.[1] The market for migratory workers is unlike that for steelworkers; the market for engineers is worlds apart from that for professional boxers. The use of the market tool is often enhanced by taking account of these differences and by distinguishing several "ideal" types of markets. A simple typology distinguishes: the *casual* labor market, which has relatively little social or institutional structure (migratory harvest labor or some types of impermanent ghetto labor); the *industrial* labor market, in which employee and employer are closely linked (basic steel or an electric power plant); and the *professional* market, where workers are identified with their careers (physicians and engineers).

These types of labor markets differ in several ways—the content of the job, or the tasks performed; the degree of attachment to any single employer (including self-employment); the extent of investment in training and education required for the job; the tendency toward a long-term career; and the amount of capital equipment associated with the labor. These differences have considerable effect upon the level of wages, stability of employment, system of information respecting job opportunities, extent of mobility and turnover, access to jobs, and other features of labor-market performance. The following table summarizes some of the main features of the three ideal types:

Table 1–1   TYPES OF LABOR MARKETS

	Casual	Industrial	Professional
Job Content	Variable and ordinarily unskilled	Narrowly defined and various levels of skill	Broadly defined and high-skill
Investment in Training	None	Medium, on the job	High
Relation to Capital	Little	Considerable	Independent, except some associated with high-capital intensity (for example, engineers)
Attachment to a Single Enterprise	None	High	Low
Career Perspective	None	Little	High

[1] ". . . . the labor market is—by nature, and quite independently of Trade Union organization —a very special kind of market, a market which is likely to develop "social" as well as purely economic aspects. The conditions for this to happen are: (1) that the worker should be free to change his employer, not being bound by any form of quasi-serfdom; (2) that employment should be regular, i.e., non-casual, so that there is a presumption that the relation between the employer and at least the major part of his employees will be a continuing relation." J.R. Hicks, *The Theory of Wages*, 2nd ed. (New York: St. Martin's, 1963), p. 317.

When considering the industrial labor market, and sometimes professionals such as teachers, it is useful to use the concept of an internal labor market to distinguish the complex movement of workers within a plant from their movement among different enterprises. The movements internal to an enterprise consist of promotions, layoffs, discharges, transfers, or retirements; they take place in accord with well-defined rules set up by management, at least in larger enterprises, or through collective bargaining agreements. The concept of an internal labor market helps to bridge the gap between economic analysis and industrial relations.

Institutional Analysis: Industrial Relations

Industrial relations adds to labor-market analysis a concern for the collective behavior of workers (usually in unions), of management associations, and of government agencies and for the issues of work rules and dispute settlement. Many problems arising within companies, including the wage and allocative rules for jobs specific to the company, are fruitfully handled in an industrial relations framework.

The main elements of a system of industrial relations are:

Industrial workers and their organizations. Industrialization creates workers whose livelihood depends on employment opportunities provided by enterprises. These workers perform under the supervision of managers for wages or salaries and other compensation such as vacations and pensions. Industrial wage and salary earners do not sell directly the product of their labor, they are not self-employed, nor do they receive significant payments in kind as in traditional agriculture. They constitute a "working class." Within the enterprise their jobs are typically arranged in hierarchical order with lines of supervision and authority, rules for promotion, and different rights with regard to layoffs. For instance, among production and maintenance workers alone, a basic steel plant in the United States may have several thousand job classifications, 31 levels of hourly wage rates, and several hundred seniority districts relevant for promotions and layoffs. At each work place, particularly in large enterprises, industrial society develops a form and order for its work force.

Organizations of workers take various forms. Some have been confined to a single locality or enterprise; others organize in many industries over a wide geographic area. The International Association of Machinists, for example, contains workers in airline companies, machine tool shops, shipyards, railroads, can factories, and so on. Industrial unions typically include most production and maintenance workers in an industry in their jurisdiction; craft unions are generally limited to a single or several related occupations.

In the United States, unions are primarily concerned with "bread and butter" issues: higher pay, more benefits, less hours, and the like. They represent workers in periodic negotiations on these and other issues. At the end of negotiations, perhaps after a strike or lockout, unions and management sign a

5

lengthy written contract formalizing the work relation. The unions also represent workers in the daily process of "living with" the contract both informally at the work place and formally through grievance procedures. Worker organizations elsewhere may have a different orientation: in France unions have often been primarily concerned with political power; those in Africa were initially concerned with expelling colonials and bringing national independence. Despite this diversity in form and purpose, organizations of workers everywhere tend to emerge in the industrialization process.

Management. Industrialization also creates managers to supervise the labor force and to direct the enterprise. The enterprise may be owned privately, by government, or by both. The management of an enterprise may have secured its position by family ties, through election by stockholders, by appointment from government or the ruling party, or (as in Yugoslavia) by decision of elected representatives of the workers and the local government. Whatever the selection procedure, industrialization is generally characterized by professional management whose selection depends on competence rather than on family or political acceptability. Large enterprises often include specialized staffs and a top-management group concerned with planning, coordinating, and appraising company development. In some situations, managements band together to form employer associations. In Sweden, for example, most employers are members of the Swedish Employers' Confederation. These associations are concerned with broad problems of national economic policy as well as with presenting a "united" front to unions.

Government agencies. Government agencies dealing with the problems and conflicts of the labor market also develop in the course of industrialization. In many situations, the government establishes rules for the work place—safety regulations, minimum wage laws—and prescribes limits of conflict and procedures for dispute settlement. When, as in the Soviet Union or in some developing countries, the government is also the dominant employer of industrial labor, its policies and actions in this respect are a critical element in the system. In other countries, including the United States and Great Britain, the government establishes only a general framework for negotiations. Management and labor organizations establish most of the rules of the work place through "collective bargaining."

Marxian Analysis

An entirely different perspective on labor problems is found in the work of Karl Marx and Marxian economists. Although Marx was concerned with the whole spectrum of economic problems, his principle focus was on the way in which economic institutions change. In Marx's view, economic systems, such as capitalism, evolve as a result of class struggles. In capitalist economies the two principal classes are capitalists, who own the tools of production, and workers, who sell their labor in the market. Marx developed his economic

6

theory to examine the relation between these classes and to predict the result of the conflict between them.

In capsule form this theory is formed from three strands of analysis:

1. *A labor theory of value.* Marx held that workers are the only source of economic value. "That which determines the magnitude of the value of any article is the amount of labor . . . or labor time socially necessary for its production."[2] This proposition has two important implications: it suggests that the prices of goods will vary in proportion to the labor time devoted to them and, more importantly, that labor "deserves" the entire national product since it alone produces economic value. As a theory of prices the labor theory has been rejected by virtually all economists, for it does not adequately account for the role of machinery in production or for the effect of demand on prices. Some modern analysts, however, view the proposition as useful in focusing attention on the class structure of capitalism and on the distribution of incomes between workers and capitalists. They accept the role of capital in the form of machinery and equipment in creating "value" and setting prices but not the role of capitalists or stockholders. "What is important is to say that owning capital is not a productive activity."[3]

2. *Internal contradictions of capitalism.* According to Marx, the normal operation of the capitalist system breeds economic catastrophe and the system's demise. In the Marxist view, capitalists continually seek to increase their share of output by cutting wages, extending hours of work, and investing in machines to reduce labor cost. Whenever demand for workers is strong and wages begin to rise, capitalists introduce *labor saving inventions* to replace workers. The workers who lose their jobs form a *reserve army of unemployed*, whose presence enables employers to cut wages to a bare minimum. As time proceeds, the economic position of workers worsens either absolutely or relative to that of capitalists. Skilled jobs disappear and the various interests and conditions of life within the ranks of the proletariat are equalized.

Paradoxically, although these actions are taken to increase capitalist profits, they create three forces which destroy the capitalist system: (1) increased monopolization of markets as larger capitalists (those with bigger investments) drive out smaller ones in bad times; (2) recurrent and continually worsening economic crises, with periods of substantial unemployment breeding discontent; (3) a *unified* working class with the incentive and capability of taking over the machinery of production. As Marx explains, it is the development of the working class, "a class always increasing in numbers, and disciplined, united, organized by the very mechanism of the process of capitalist production"[4] that spells the end of the system. The workers eventually revolt, possibly under the leadership of a communist party, and create a new society.

---

[2] K. Marx, *Capital: A Critique of Political Economy,* Volume 1.

[3] J. Robinson, "An Essay on Marxist Economics," (New York: MacMillan, 1966), p. 18.

[4] *Capital:* Volume I.

3. The nature of communist society. Although Marx did not examine carefully the operation of the post-capitalist economic system, the idea of a socialist or communist world in which classes merge into a single body politic has been one of the chief attractions of his system. In the new communist society men are not obligated to sell labor to others in the market; society rather than markets regulates production; there is no capitalist class "exploiting" workers. Ultimately, the problems of labor are determined by the rule "from each according to his ability, to each according to his needs," rather than by the rules of market economics.

In one form or another, Marxian ideas have been extremely influential in the thinking of intellectuals, labor leaders, and workers. The dual attraction of a critique of capitalist economies and the promise of socialist paradise has appealed to persons throughout the world. In Europe, Marxism was important in the pre-Hitler German trade unions and is important in the French and Italian labor movements. In post-World-War-II Japan the political protest of one major labor federation finds its base in a version of Marxian ideas. And in many less-developed countries, one finds large numbers of labor organizations and politicians influenced at least in part by these ideas.

There are both theoretical and empirical problems with the Marxian picture of labor developments. As noted, the labor theory of value does not adequately account for the role of machinery in producing commodities and is a poor indicator of relative prices. Technological progress and additional machinery have not created a "reserve army of unemployed" nor, on balance, destroyed skilled jobs; the income of workers has increased, not declined, over time. Finally, the working class does not constitute a unified revolutionary group in advanced capitalist countries today.

Despite, or perhaps because of, these inconsistencies, knowledge of Marxian theory can add to an understanding of labor problems. On one hand, the Marxian view directs attention to issues that are often otherwise neglected: the social relations arising from the sale of labor as a commodity in the market; the connections between market position and political power; the economic rationale of income distribution; possible deleterious effects of technological change on the number and quality of jobs; and the evolution of labor market institutions. On the other hand, it is important to understand where Marx went wrong—to determine the economic and social forces which invalidated many of his predictions.

Labor and Theories of History

The importance of labor-market activity in the life of industrial economies has given labor problems a central position in many theories of human history. Marx's interpretation of history as a struggle between classes defined by their opposition in the labor market is the most famous of these theories. The Marxian analysis depends critically, as we have seen, on the market creating a unified working class with the incentive and power to overthrow capitalism. Other theorists have identified different groups as the strategic force in industrial societies. To Thorstein Veblen, for example, highly trained engineers rather than unskilled workers were the logical group to revolutionize society. In *Engineers and the Price System*. Veblen argued that modern technology makes engineers indispensable and capitalists dispensable and suggested that engineers might arise and overthrow the business interests. The result would be a new society based on engineering efficiency rather than on the logic of the price system. In the years immediately following World War II, other observers, fascinated by the rise of powerful industrial unions, believed that unions were going to dominate society. Union power, it was suggested, would destroy the price system and create a syndicalist world in which unions and management would jointly decide on output, employment, wages, and prices, free from present market pressures and consumer preferences. More recently, Professor John Kenneth Galbraith has focused on the role of specialized manpower, including high-level management, industrial scientists, and engineers in the economic and political life of the United States. "Trained and educated manpower . . . [has] now [become] the decisive factor of production."[5] According to Galbraith, the specialists constitute a new class, the *technostructure*, that plans and manages both the production of goods and consumer desires to achieve rapid economic growth, often at the expense of the quality of life. At the same time, however, the need for intellectual specialists places great potential power in the hands of educators and nonindustrial scientists who, Galbraith hopes, will form a new class that assumes the responsibility for political leadership.

From the perspective of labor economics, the characteristic feature of each of these theories is the assumption that occupational status—as worker, engineer, or educator—defines the role of persons in history. Religious, racial, national, and political distinctions are ignored in favor of occupational distinctions. The crusades of industrial society are expected to be crusades of workers against capitalists, engineers against financiers, educators against the technostructure—not crusades of Christians or Muslims, Cavaliers or Roundheads, Germans or French.

Not surprisingly, each of these grand theories focuses on a specific characteristic of industrial life and extrapolates it into the future. Marx, for example, generalized from his observations of the effect of the Industrial Revolution on British workers; Veblen, on the increased technical complexity of the industrial process in the era of World War I and the onset of movements like that of scientific management; Galbraith, on the increased industrial employment of specialists and professional managers and the growth of the education sector. The historical evidence suggests that extrapolations of this kind are hazardous, for economic and social forces rarely proceed at a steady pace in the same direction; occupations or classes which are growing today may taper off in the

9

[5] J.K. Galbraith, *The New Industrial State* (Boston: Houghton-Mifflin, 1968), p. 391.

future and new groups may arise from changes in technology or consumer taste. Classes of persons, such as industrial workers, may become differentiated into diverse specialized groups, with differing interests, life styles, and economic status. More fundamentally, perhaps, the grand theories often minimize the importance of competition in the labor market between persons in the same field— a competition for jobs, income, and prestige which fragments groups that are expected to form a unified class.

Structure of the Book

Succeeding chapters of this book use the tools of market analysis and industrial relations to analyze the principal problems of the labor market—those of wage determination, employment and unemployment, job skills, industrial conflict and so on. The principal tool in chapters Two to Five is the theory of markets. Here we examine the influence of economic incentives on the supply decisions of individuals—on whether they seek work in the market, the skills they obtain, the job they choose—and on the employment decisions of firms. One of the main themes in these chapters is the way in which the decisions of large numbers of suppliers and firms interact to determine an equilibrium level of wages and employment.

Chapters Six and Seven, on the other hand, make extensive use of the principles of industrial relations. The issues considered include the functioning of collective bargaining between unions and management in the United States; the role of the law in regulating labor institutions and processes; the rules of the work place. To show the diverse institutional arrangements that can be used to structure the labor market, Chapter Seven describes the industrial relations systems of three countries other than the United States: Japan, Russia, and Yugoslavia.

Selected Readings

Ashton, T. S., *The Industrial Revolution, 1760–1830*. London: Oxford University Press, 1948.

Hobsbawn, E. J., *Labouring Men: Studies in the History of Labor*. New York: Anchor, 1968

Kerr, Clark; Dunlop, John T.; Harbison, Frederick; and Myers, Charles A.; *Industrialism and Industrial Man, The Problems of Labor and Management in Economic Growth*. New York: Oxford University Press, 1964.

Kuznets, S., *Modern Economic Growth*. New Haven: Yale University Press, 1966.

Marx, Karl, *Capital*, Vol. I, Chapter XV.

Shostak, Arthur B., *Blue-Collar Life*. New York: Random House, 1969.

Sweezy, P., *The Theory of Capitalist Development*. London: Dobson, 1962.

Labor Supply

and Unemployment

CHAPTER TWO

Human work is society's largest productive resource and one of the most important activities in the life of almost everyone. Approximately 70 percent of the national income of the United States is paid to workers for their contribution to production. More than two-thirds of American adults work at some time during a normal year. For many, more hours are spent on the job than in any other activity.

What factors determine the amount of human work available in a society? What explains the number of people in the labor force and the time they devote to work? Why do some people end up unemployed?

THE ELEMENTS OF LABOR SUPPLY

The amount of labor which is available to an economy depends on:

1. The size and composition of the population
2. The proportion of the population willing to work
3. The length of the work week
4. The number of weeks worked compared to those spent on vacations or holidays
5. The intensity of the work effort
6. The education and training of the work force.[1]

[1] Education and training are discussed in the next chapter.

Taken together, these six elements define the total supply of human work which can be used to produce goods and services in the market. This supply is not fixed in an economy, even in short periods of time. Each of these elements is the result of the decisions of millions of individuals and households, who are influenced by the economic incentives of wages and job availability as well as by custom, taste, and ability. Each person must decide how much time and effort to allocate to the labor market and how much to spend on other activities, such as leisure, education, working in the home[2], and so on. Each must choose from among the feasible alternatives a level of education, a career, and a style of working life.

The relationship between the work offered by persons and economic incentive defines a *supply curve* of labor. As a first approximation it is convenient to think of each dimension of supply as dependent on wages. Since incentives include working conditions and nonmonetary factors, in addition to wages, this is a simplification of actual behavior. It is an example of the *ceteris paribus* ("other things remaining unchanged") assumption which is an essential first step in the investigation of complex problems.

Supply Curves

Because the supply curve is a fundamental tool in labor market analysis, we shall examine first several important supply relations. Fig. 2–1 depicts graphically the four types of supply curves that are most useful in describing real-world behavior. What is the meaning of these curves? What behavior do they represent?

The first curve (A) is horizontal. It tells us that at the wage W_o as much work is available as could possibly be desired. At wages below W_o no work is supplied at all; at wages above W_o there is no increase in supply.

There are several situations for which this *infinitely elastic* supply function represents behavior in the labor market. If the horizontal axis measures total population, the curve represents the long-run supply of population posited by Reverend Malthus in the 1760's. According to Malthus, the production of babies depends on the standard of living, which is set by the wage rate. When the wage is high, exceeding a "subsistence level," the production of babies increases and population grows. The larger population eventually leads to an increased supply of workers, which drives wages down to the subsistence level. In the diagram, W_o is subsistence wage. If the wage exceeds W_o *in the short run*, the growth of population eventually drives the wage down to W_o; if the wage is below W_o, famine and disease eventually cause the population to decline, raising the wage to W.

Alternatively, the supply of labor in less-developed countries is often

---

[2]Working in the home is exceedingly important for women in current society. Recent work by Professor Gary S. Becker and his colleagues deals with the role of women in producing goods and services in the home. See G. Becker, *Economic Theory* (New York: Knopf, 1971).

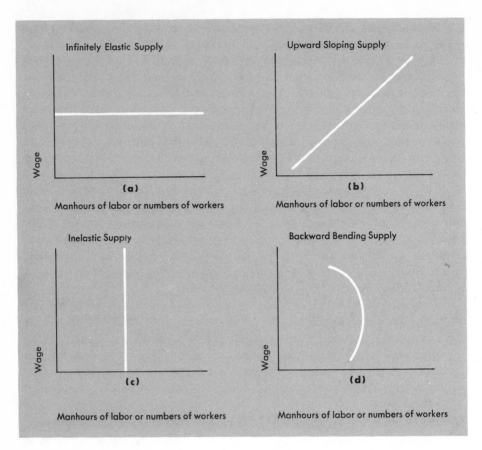

FIG. 2–1 Labor supply curves.

viewed as infinitely elastic. Some development specialists, notably Professor W. A. Lewis of Princeton, believe that less-developed countries have an *unlimited* supply of labor to the modern sector at a particular wage (for instance, W_o in the figure).[3] Supply is unlimited, at least for many years, because of the existence of "underemployed" persons in traditional agricultural, household, or trading activities. These individuals have very low incomes and are thus willing to accept work at W_o when jobs are created in the modern sector. If the supply of labor to the modern sector is measured along the horizontal axis, the figure depicts this type of labor condition.

Finally, in a competitive market the supply of workers to individual firms can also be viewed as infinitely elastic. At the "going wage rate" W_o, the com-

[3]W.A. Lewis, "Economic Development with Unlimited Supplies of Labor," (Journal Article, *Manchester School of Economic and Social Studies*, May 1954).

petitive firm is assumed to be able to hire as many workers as are needed. The firm is too small to influence the wage rate in the market.

The supply curve of workers to an entire industry or occupation, on the other hand, is likely to have a different shape. In this case, more persons will offer their services when wages increase (relative to those elsewhere) and less when they decrease. Supply curve B depicts such a situation; supply is upward sloping, with a positive elasticity.[4] The greater the elasticity the smaller is the change in wages needed to draw a given number of workers into or out of an industry or occupation.

Another case to consider is when wages have *no effect* on the quantity of work supplied. Complete inelasticity of supply (shown in curve C) may be relevant to short-run situations when individuals do not have time to adjust their work plans or to occupations requiring great training, where supply is primarily determined by past rather than current economic conditions. It also describes an economy making full use of its labor resources. When individuals are supplying the maximum amount of work that they are willing to offer, increases in wages will be unable to draw forth more work.

One additional supply relation deserves attention. This is the famous "backward bending supply of labor" shown by curve D. Here, an increase in wages (beyond W_o) reduces the amount of work offered. Decisions regarding hours of work may be represented by such a relation, for it often happens that increases in wages per hour (which permits the same income with less work) reduce the number of hours worked—a phenomenon examined in detail later. Increases in wages lead to less work when persons are working with a fixed money goal in mind, for instance to buy a $200 used car.

STUDY OF SUPPLY

The differently shaped supply curves represent, we have seen, different types of market behavior. To understand developments in the labor market, to predict the future, or to devise workable manpower policy, it is important to know the behavior characteristic of each of the dimensions of supply. For example, does the number of individuals seeking work increase or decrease when jobs are scarce? What is the effect of increased incomes on the work decisions of married women? Will more wives enter the labor force in the future? What explains the historic shortening of the work week? Will the number of hours decline to 30 or 35 hours per week in the future as income grows? What effects do changing wages have on work incentive? Will the increase in the number of individuals preparing for professional and managerial jobs continue? All these

[4]The *elasticity* of a supply curve is the percentage change in the number of persons offering to work per one percent change in wages. Algebraically, if N=number of workers and W=wages, then elasticity is defined as % change N/% change W.

questions require knowledge of the elasticity of supply curves at a particular time or likely shifts in the curves over time.

Measures of Supply: The Labor Force and Labor Participation Rates

A first step in measuring the supply of labor in an economy is to count the number of persons willing to work in a specified time period. The Bureau of Census classifies individuals as members of the *labor force* if (a) they are employed or (b) are without work and actively seeking employment during the period of the labor-force survey.[5] The latter group are counted as unemployed, whereas adults without a job and not interested in working in the market, including homemakers, students, and others, are "not in the labor force." The proportion of persons in the labor force (employed and unemployed) to the total population defines a *labor force participation rate*. The rate varies greatly among different subgroups of the total population: 97.1 percent of males between 25 and 54 are in the labor force compared to less than 50 percent of similarly aged females.

The total labor force in the United States includes diverse groups of individuals, whose number depends on the population in the group and its participation rate (Table 2–1). One-third of the labor force is made up of "prime age" males, 25 to 54 years old; another third are females, mostly middle-aged wives; approximately one in ten are nonwhites, many recent migrants from Southern farms to Northern cities. A relatively great proportion of the nonwhite work force are females or young males.

As the structure of population and labor participation rates change, the composition of the work force changes. For the decade of the 1970's the principal changes expected by the Bureau of Census are a substantial increase in the number of male workers aged 25 to 34 and a great increase in the female work force in all age brackets (Table 2–1).

Why are these changes expected? The increase in men aged 25 to 34 is traceable to the ups and downs of birth rates. Low birth rates in the Depression produced a very small number of persons of this age in 1968, whereas the post-World-War-II baby boom will yield a large number in 1980. Since virtually all men aged 25 to 34 participate in the labor force, knowledge of the future size of the group provides a relatively accurate projection of the available work force.[6]

The predicted change in the female labor force or in the number of young or old male workers involves more complex considerations, for the labor force rates of these groups change over time. Historically, the participation of young

[5]The Census makes a sample survey of 50,000 households each month. For a description of the concepts and procedures used see the appendix to the monthly publication, *Employment and Earnings* (United States Department of Labor).

[6]Immigration should also be considered. Barring change in the laws, it is not too difficult to adjust projections for the anticipated number of future immigrant males, 25 to 34 years old.

Table 2–1   THE AMERICAN LABOR FORCE,
ACTUAL 1968 TO PROJECTED 1980

	Actual Figures 1968			Projected Figures, 1980	
	Population (thousands)	Labor Force Participation	Number in Labor Force	Number in Labor Force	Percentage Change
Male 16+	65,307	81.2	53,030	64,061	13%
16–24	15,042	73.0	10,983	13,888	26%
25–34	11,715	97.1	11,376	17,590	55%
35–44	11,442	97.2	11,122	12,084	9%
45–64	19,258	90.3	17,394	18,403	6%
65+	7,890	27.3	2,154	2,096	−3%
Female 16+	70,293	41.6	29,242	35,881	23%
16–24	14,806	47.9	7,199	8,666	20%
25–34	11,993	42.6	5,104	7,347	44%
35–44	12,002	48.9	5,869	6,386	9%
45–64	20,995	47.9	10,070	12,142	21%
65+	10,406	9.6	999	1,340	33%

Source: U.S. Department of Labor.

men and men over 65 in the labor force has *declined*, whereas the participation of women, especially married women, has increased dramatically. Between 1890 and 1968, for example, the fraction of men aged 14 to 19 in the labor force fell from 57 percent to 44 percent, the fraction of men over 65 in the labor force fell from 74 percent to 27 percent. During the same period, female participation increased from 18 percent to nearly 40 percent.

The Bureau of Census projections are based on the assumption that these trends will continue into the future: the participation rate of women is expected to reach 42 percent in 1980, the rate for older men to drop to 22 percent, and that for the young males is supposed to remain roughly fixed.

Participation Behavior

Differences in the labor-force participation behavior among prime-age males, older men, young boys, and women are best understood in the context of the economic forces affecting these diverse groups. In our society, prime-age males are the chief breadwinners of families and thus are permanent members of the labor force, working or seeking work throughout the year.[7] Most older or younger men and most women, on the other hand, are not normally the main source of family income. As a result they have greater *discretion* in their work decisions and constitute a *secondary labor force* whose size varies in response

[7] As might be expected, a woman, young man, or older man who is the chief breadwinner in a household is more likely to be in the labor force than one who is not the principal breadwinner. Single women aged 25 to 34. for instance, have a participation rate of 80.9 whereas their married counterparts' rate is only 35.0.

to economic and social conditions. Many conditions have altered the participation rate of young males, older males, and women in years past (Figure 2–2).

The increased significance of education in the job market and the concomitant growth of high school and college training are the main factors behind the downward trend in the participation of young males. Persons enrolled in school are less likely to be in the labor force, especially during the school season, than other people.

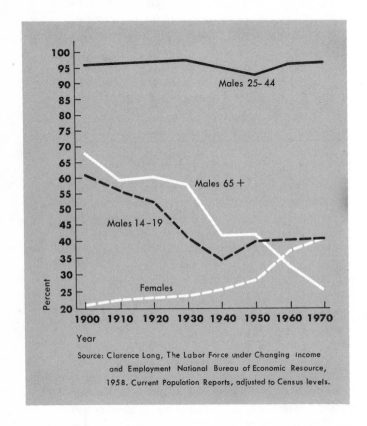

Source: Clarence Long, The Labor Force under Changing Income and Employment National Bureau of Economic Resource, 1958. Current Population Reports, adjusted to Census levels.

FIG. 2–2 Trends in labor force participation, 1900-1970.

The remarkable increase in female participation, which is centered among married women in the 35 to 54 age bracket, is more difficult to explain. Husbands today earn about three times as much in real income as in the 1890's. Why haven't wives consumed this income with additional leisure instead of seeking work?

One factor that has acted to increase female participation rates is the enormous expansion of the amount and quality of household appliances, factory-made clothing and prepackaged food. These improvements in the technology of

18

the household reduce the amount of time that women devote to housekeeping and thus permit them to seek work. In a sense, employment in the market is substituted for employment at home.

Substantial increases in the wages offered to women due in part to the growth of output in the industries that employ them also contribute to the increase in participation. Of especially great significance is the flexibility of American employers in offering part-time jobs to women who are available for only a few hours a day. From 1952 to 1969 the number of part-time jobs grew by 63 percent compared to an increase of just 18 percent in full-time positions. Without this shift in the nature of employment opportunities many women would be unable to work.

Finally, female employment has increased as employers have substituted women for men in many office and sales jobs. In 1910, for instance, one out of four clerical or sales workers was female; in 1960 more than half of these workers were female. Typing, sales, stenography, bookkeeping, operating a telephone switchboard, elementary and secondary school teaching are jobs of this kind.[8]

The secular decline in participation of older men is as striking as is the increase in female participation. Even in the past 20 years the retirement of older men from work has been dramatic: in 1947 48 percent of men 65 or older were in the labor force whereas in 1960 only 27 percent participated in the labor market. Two factors have been at work here. In part, the decline is a voluntary response to the retirement provisions of Social Security and private pension programs. Receipt of Social Security and most private payments after 65 is contingent on cessation of work paying more than nominal amounts. As payments under these plans have increased over time, older men have had increased incentive to withdraw from the labor force.

Compulsory retirement policies of employers also have a substantial impact on the retirement decision, with at least one in five retirees in the mid-1960's forced out of the labor force by employer requirements. The merits and demerits of compulsory retirement rules are complex. Many employers believe that the skills of older workers are outmoded by technological advance and that they are less able to learn new jobs than younger men. Under most union agreements and in many other cases, moreover, promotion depends significantly on seniority, so that older men must be "pushed aside" to permit promotion of the young. On the other hand, forcing a man to retire is a costly and coercive solution to the problems of age—it inactivates many potentially productive persons who would prefer to work. Perhaps a system of partial demotion for less-productive older workers and the relaxation of Social Security provisions against

---

[8]The improvement in employment opportunities in the market place as compared to the home can be summarized in terms of wages. The wages offered women working for employers have increased relative to those for working at home, which motivates a shift into the market.

working after 65 would offer older persons a better set of options than exist today, particularly in light of the great differences in health, vitality, and productivity that exist among employees aged 65 and over.

Secondary workers adjust their labor-force behavior to *cyclical* changes in the availability of jobs as well as to long-term economic and social developments. When the economy is booming and the number of jobs increases, *more* secondary workers seek employment than under "normal" conditions. When the economy suffers from a recession and a decrease in employment, *fewer* secondary workers search for work. On the average, it has been estimated that for every ten jobs created, an additional two or three workers will be drawn into the labor force. Analogously, for every ten jobs disappearing in a recession, two to three potential workers will withdraw from the labor force.[9]

The observed cyclic changes in the size of the labor force are the net result of opposing forms of behavior. In a recession, some members of the secondary labor force are *discouraged* by the scarcity of jobs and withdraw from the market. Other persons are forced by the loss of employment of the chief breadwinner of their family to seek work. In localities suffering from a chronic lack of jobs for men, as in some New England textile and shoe towns in the 1950's, *additional* worker behavior may increase the secondary labor force considerably. When the economy prospers, discouraged workers re-enter the market, swelling the labor force; additional workers leave when the head of their household obtains work.

Overall, discouraged worker behavior dominates the change in participation over the business cycle. It is not difficult to see why. Even in a recession, the vast majority of heads of households remain employed. The discouragement of job scarcity thus affects many more persons than the incentive to replace breadwinners in the markets. In prosperous times, also, more persons are affected by the pull of employment opportunities than by the added employment of primary workers.

The sensitivity of the labor force to changes in economic conditions creates problems in interpreting statistical measures of total unemployment. Since fewer people seek jobs when they are scarce, the measured unemployment in a recession understates the amount of unused labor resources. It fails to account for persons who would enter the market if jobs were available—the

---

[9] J. Mincer, "Labor Force Participation and Unemployment: A Review of Recent Evidence," in R. A. Gordon and M. S. Gordon, *Prosperity and Unemployment* (New York: John Wiley, 1966), pp. 73–112.

"disguised" or "hidden" unemployed. If these persons were counted as part of the unemployed the measured rate would increase by one or two percentage points above the five to six percent of recent recessions. The unemployment problem would look much worse.

Although some adjustment for the cyclic change in the size of the labor force is needed to get a true notion of unused resources, the significance of hidden unemployment should not be overstated. Most of the persons pushed out of the work force by job scarcity are secondary workers whose failure to obtain work—whether it shows up in increased unemployment or reduced participation—is not comparable to the unemployment of heads of households. In terms of human well-being, it is very different for a 35-year-old man supporting a family to be unemployed than for a secondary worker—say, a woman or a male student who wants to earn a few dollars before the Christmas holidays— to withdraw from the market because of job scarcity. In evaluating the cost of unemployment it is important to consider the composition as well as the total level of the measured and disguised unemployed.

Other Dimensions of Labor Supply: Hours and Weeks Worked

The number of hours worked per week and the time spent on vacation and holidays also determine the available supply of human labor.

Historically, the workweek has been shortened drastically. In 1840, the average person worked 70 to 80 hours per week in the United States. Today the *scheduled workweek* is generally 40 hours, lower in a few industries such as printing, brewing, and in many office occupations in metropolitan areas. Most of the decline to 40 hours occurred prior to 1940, with the length of the average workweek stabilizing at 40 hours in the post-World-War-II period.

An *average* scheduled work week of 40 hours does not mean that everyone works just 40 hours each week. When the economy is booming, employers offer *overtime* work at premium rates. Under the Fair Labor Standards Act (1938), which established the 40-hour week (and also the minimum wage), workers must be paid at least one and one-half times their normal rate of pay for hours beyond 40. Collective bargaining agreements provide for overtime rates that are sometimes higher and also typically specify overtime for hours worked beyond the scheduled workday. Most workers accept the opportunity to work at these rates. In 1966, overtime hours raised the average total hours of production workers in manufacturing to 41.4 per week. In some kinds of work, moreover, it is normal for the workweek to differ from 40 hours. University professors, doctors, lawyers, and independent professionals have considerable leeway in their workweek. The professor, for instance, is obligated to appear in class for perhaps six to fifteen hours per week—although of course he works many hours beyond this (42.3 hours in total, according to the *Census of Population*).   **21**

The doctor averages 57.3 hours per week. By law, the airline pilot is limited to 85 hours of flying during a month, although other duties increase the total working time.

While the average workweek has been relatively fixed since World War II, the number of days devoted to holidays or vacations has increased. In 1959, just 27 percent of plant and 38 percent of office workers with the needed years of seniority received three or more weeks of paid vacation; in 1967 more than half the plant work force and two-thirds of office workers enjoyed such benefits. The cost to major companies of "time not worked" jumped from 5½ percent of total payroll lost in 1947 to 10 percent in 1967. In some pacesetting industries, moreover, holiday or vacation time exceeds the economy-wide average. Steelworkers, for example, have bargained for a "sabbatical program" similar to that given professors. Under this plan, a long-service worker who meets certain requirements receives a three-month vacation with pay every five years in addition to his normal vacation.

The net result of the pre-1940 decline in the length of the workweek and the more-recent increase in vacation and holiday time is that an employee today contributes about 2000 hours of work during the year, compared to perhaps 2700 hours in the early 1900's. Because individuals are also likely to enter the work force at a later age than in the 1900's and to retire earlier, the hours of work contributed during the lifetime have dropped even more dramatically. Some of the fruits of the twentieth-century economic growth have been taken in increased leisure.

Analysis of Work–Leisure Decisions

The average work load per employee did not have to decrease by some 700 hours per year. Conceivably, workers could have chosen greater income exclusively, rather than some increased leisure during economic growth. At current wage rates (about $3.50 per hour in 1971) a worker might make $2450 more per year by working as many hours as the 1909 worker. Indeed, a sizable number of Americans work in excess of 40 hours per week. Some work overtime, whereas others "moonlight"—hold one 40-hour job and one or more additional jobs.

Why have most Americans chosen to decrease the hours of work over time as wages have increased? Why do most workers accept overtime and some workers moonlight?

An increase in wages has, according to economic theory, two effects on a worker: an *income effect* and a *substitution effect*. The income effect is based on the obvious fact that an increase in wages makes you wealthier. Without any change in hours worked, your income is higher. But what do you do when your income is higher? Probably use the additional money to buy a new coat, a record album, and a season's ticket to the theatre (or some other collection of consumer goods). In addition, however, you are likely to want *more leisure or consumption time* to enjoy your increased affluence. But leisure is a funny commodity, for it can be bought in only one way—by working fewer hours! Thus, when wages increase, the income effect operates to reduce working time.

The substitution effect works in the opposite direction. It is based on the fact that an increase in wages makes leisure time *more expensive* than in the past. After all, leisure is not "free"—an hour spent in leisure could be devoted to work, and working rewards you at the wage rate. But this means that an increase in the wage rate increases the price of leisure, and when a price goes up, you purchase less. When wages increase, the substitution effect operates to reduce leisure time and increase working time. The ultimate impact of a wage increase on the number of hours worked depends on the net effect of these forces. When the substitution effect is greater than the income effect, the number of hours increases in response to a wage increase; when the income effect is greater, the hours decrease and we have a *backward-bending* supply curve like that of Fig. 3–1D.

Past declines in the number of hours worked over the year have accompanied substantial wage gains. This indicates that *overall* the income effect has dominated the substitution effect in past years.

The apparent dominance of the income effect is consistent with the acceptance of overtime work, for the premium paid for overtime is received only for hours worked in excess of 40 hours. Hence, the income effect associated with increased wages does not operate unless the worker accepts overtime. The substitution effect is crucial in the decision to work overtime or to moonlight because the higher wage is received *only* for the extra hour of work.

Intensity of Work Effort and Productivity

The effect of work intensity on the supply of labor available to society is clear-cut: a healthy, hard-working individual contributes more to output and is thus more productive than an individual working below his capacity or one with below-normal capacity or low morale. In effect, the supply of labor is greater, the more willing and able persons are to do their jobs. The intensity of the work effort is affected by many factors, including:

1. The physical condition of the worker. In less-developed countries the physical condition of workers seems to be an exceedingly important determinant of their effectiveness. One study of the rate of growth of labor productivity (output per man-hour worked) in such countries found, for example, that improvement in health associated with increased calories per worker was the major determinant of greater productivity in the period from 1950 to 1960.[10]

---

[10]W. Galenson and G. Pratt., *The Quality of Labor and Economic Development in Certain Countries, A Preliminary Study* (Geneva: International Labor Organization, 1964).

Another study estimated that the loss of working time due to sickness in countries such as Burma and Ecuador was in the area of 13 to 15 percent of available work hours. By contrast, in the United States, sickness reduces working time by perhaps 3 percent.[11]

2. Methods of wage payment. Economics points out the effect of various methods of wage payment on motivation and efficiency. There are at least three basic ways to pay workers:

> *Time rates*—a certain number of dollars per hour, week, or month.
>
> *Piecework incentive rates*—dollars per unit of output produced by an individual, usually with a guaranteed minimum.
>
> *Group incentive rates*—payment based on the output of a particular working group or plant, possibly based on the profits of the enterprise.

Variants of these methods of wage payment are used throughout the world. In the U.S.S.R., piecework predominates; in Yugoslavia, group incentives in the form of profit sharing. In the United States, more than three-fourths of the work force is paid by hourly rates.

These alternatives tend to be associated with different types and intensities of supervision of the work force. Time rates are probably most frequently used when workers have little control over the pace of work, as in continuous operation plants such as oil refineries and electric generating stations, or when it is possible to increase output and beat an incentive system by sacrificing the quality of goods. Piece rates are generally successful under the opposite circumstances: when workers determine the intensity of work and production consists of easily measured standard outputs. Even under these conditions, however, it is often difficult to devise a well-functioning piece-rate system. Workers may fear cuts in rates if they produce at full capacity and thereby restrict rather than speed up production. Technological change, caused perhaps by new machinery, may destroy the logic of a piecework system by raising productivity so much that earnings jump out of line with earnings in comparable jobs elsewhere in the plant or industry, necessitating a revision of the incentive system.

Group incentive plans face similar problems, with profit sharing being the most difficult system to implement. Since profits depend on the demand for output and on managerial decision making as well as worker efficiency, it is not possible to attribute high or low profits to the behavior of workers alone. The Kaiser Steel Program, one of the best-known group incentive plans in the United States, tries to circumvent this problem by tying workers' receipts to the cost savings attributable to improved use of materials and increased labor productivity rather than to profits per se.

3. Motivation and morale. Worker motivation is a complex subject, calling

[11]H. Correa, *The Economics of Human Resources* (Amsterdam: North-Holland, 1963).

for psychological and sociological as well as economic analyses. Every manager and union representative becomes aware that workers do not always work to the limits of their capability, even recognizing that the optimum pace of work for a lifetime is different than that for a few weeks or months. Managers everywhere come to realize that the work place is seldom unorganized, in the sense that workers who continue to work together over a period often establish their own norms of conduct and their own standards of behavior and output. The work place is a social group.

Managers seek to find payment plans, methods of management, and procedures in organizing the work place which elicit greater productivity from workers and immediate supervisors. The participation of workers in many work-level decisions, the redesign of jobs to include more variety and less routine work, and the provision of various social services are illustrative of the range of efforts made to improve morale, loyalty, and involvement of workers in increasing total productivity. Some of these efforts have been made through collective bargaining[12] and others have been made by management alone. The potentials of increasing the effective supply of labor through these means are not well understood.

Unemployment

Not everyone who seeks work ends up with a job. Some persons, an average of 2.5 to 3 million in recent years, cannot find an employer willing to hire them under existing economic conditions and are counted as unemployed. Others, as we have seen, become discouraged and forsake the job hunt. The percentage of persons who are unemployed or who leave the labor force varies over the business cycle, rising in recessions or depressions and falling in booms.

The highest unemployment rate in American history was recorded in the Great Depression of the 1930's. More than 25 percent of the work force could not find jobs; many despaired of ever working again. "Some communities and industries suffered almost total devastation. . . . Williamson County, Illinois, provided almost no employment. In the town of Caello, with a population of 1350 . . . only two persons had jobs. . . . Dorora, Pennsylvania, in March, 1932, had 277 persons employed out of a population of 13,900. . . . Of the 108,000 wage and salary earners in the congressional district including Birmingham, Alabama, 22,500 were totally jobless on January 5, 1932, and 60,000 to 75,000 others were on short time. When the city advertised for 700 laborers to do 'the hard, dirty work of digging a canal at $2 for a ten-hour day,' there were over 12,000 applicants. . . ."[13] In April, 1935, the number of full-time employees at the United States Steel Company, which had a work force of a

[12]See William Gomberg, "Special Study Committees," in *Frontiers of Collective Bargaining*, John T. Dunlop and Neil W. Chamberlain, eds. (New York: Harper and Row, 1967), pp. 235–51.

[13]Irving Bernstein, *The Lean Years, A History of the American Worker, 1920–1933* (Boston: Houghton Mifflin, 1960), p. 317.

25

quarter of a million before the Depression, fell to zero; only half as many part-time workers held jobs as were fully employed four years earlier.

The Great Depression was a cataclysmic event in American economic and political history, shaping the social and political attitudes of millions of persons for years to come. Massive unemployment became almost universally viewed as the greatest economic disease of a free-enterprise system. The necessity for major countercyclical programs on the part of the federal government was recognized. The determination of the American people to avoid future economic collapse and mass joblessness is codified in the Employment Act of 1946 which proclaims "the continuing policy and responsibility of the federal government to use all practicable means consistent with . . . other essential considerations of national policy . . . to promote maximum employment. . . ."

The Meaning of Full Employment

Although unemployment has not approached the levels of the Great Depression in succeeding years, the rate of joblessness has been noticeably above zero. Even in 1953 when unemployment was at its post-World-War-II minimum, 2.9 percent of the labor force, or 1.8 million persons, were unemployed. Does this mean that the United States has never attained the goal of maximum or full employment? What is the meaning of full employment?

It is easier to state what full employment is not than what it is. It is not zero unemployment. At all times some persons enter the labor market looking for their first job; others leave an employer in search of improved income or working conditions. At all times some firms reduce output or go out of business and lay off or discharge workers. These movements of workers are a necessary feature of a dynamic economy in which employment opportunities and the individuals' seeking work change over time. As long as the period of searching for a job is reasonably short and the persons in the unemployment pool are changing rapidly—as A finds a job while B loses or quits his—the hardship of unemployment is relatively slight. In a free labor market, where the decision to seek work, to change jobs, to hire someone, or to fire someone is in the hands of individual workers and employers, it is not possible or desirable to eliminate *frictional unemployment* of this kind. Perhaps the best definition of full employment is that virtually all unemployment is frictional, a short interlude between jobs.[14]

There is no absolute criterion for determining the length of this short interlude. Is one month of unemployment frictional or a more serious matter? What

[14]At full employment, so defined, there would also be a number of job vacancies, that is, jobs which employers are trying to fill at prevailing wage rates for which they can find no takers in a reasonable period. The want-ads of newspapers and the files of the Employment Service and private employment agencies provide illustrations of these vacancies, although many vacancies may never be formally reported to outsiders. In some communities in 1967–69 the number of job vacancies appear to have been almost equal to the numbers unemployed. An alternative definition of full employment might be the situation in which job vacancies just equal the number of unemployed.

about two months? Or three? What if an individual is very choosy and refuses jobs to wait and wait and wait for the "right one"? Although a precise boundary between frictional and nonfrictional unemployment is difficult to draw, there is general agreement about the kinds and levels of unemployment that are to be viewed with concern. Almost everyone would agree that unemployment lasting three or six months or longer is not a short interlude between jobs. Most everyone would agree that the temporary unemployment of a teenager seeking a first job is less significant than an equivalent period of unemployment of heads of households. Probably we would be willing to view longer periods of unemployment as frictional if unemployment compensation payments were higher and the coverage of unemployment insurance greater. In terms of the national rate of unemployment, most economists believe that the rate should be 4 percent or less to be consistent with full employment; some place it at 3 percent or even below. If we were to take the average number of persons "unemployed one month but finding work in the next month" as a rough index of frictional unemployment, the rate would be much lower, in the area of 1.6 percent of the total work force. Other definitions of frictional unemployment, yielding a higher figure, would include explicit allowances for the seasonal character of employment in many industries and for continuing structural shifts in job opportunities among regions and industries in a dynamic economy.

The Unemployment Record, 1947–1970

Whatever the benchmark of full employment, the unemployment record since World War II is not especially good (Fig. 2–3). On four occasions, downturns in the business cycle raised the unemployment rate for the total work force to levels unacceptable to most citizens. In 1949 unemployment averaged 5.9 percent of the labor force; in 1954, 5.5 percent; in 1958, 6.8 percent; in 1961, 6.7 percent; and in early 1971, 6.1 percent. Equally troublesome was the failure of the economy to generate enough jobs in the years following the 1958 recession to restore the low levels of unemployment normally found in "good times." In 1959 and 1960, and from 1962 to 1964, unemployment averaged above 5.5 percent per annum . . . a level which compares unfavorably with past experience and policy objectives. The record of unemployment in the United States was, as can be seen in Table 2–2, among the least satisfactory in the Western world.

The principal cause for the cyclic unemployment of the post-World-War-II period and the high unemployment of 1958–64 and of 1969–70 was a general failure of businesses, consumers, and government to purchase enough goods and services to employ all men and machines at prevailing rates of pay. The technical term for this phenomenon is *inadequate aggregate demand*. Essentially the demand for output is below the level needed to create the number of jobs for full employment.

27

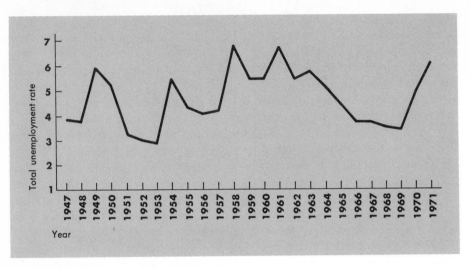

FIG. 2–3 Unemployment in the United States, 1947–1971. *Source:* U.S. Department of Labor *Handbook of Labour Statistics* (1970).

When an economy suffers from inadequate aggregate demand, general fiscal and monetary policies are needed to increase the amount of money available for spending. Increased consumer spending will induce businesses to expand production and hire more workers. Increased government spending or business investment will have a similar effect. Increases in the supply of money are also likely to have an expansionary impact on the economy and thus reduce unemployment. The eventual recovery of the United States economy from the high unemployment rates of the early 1960's can be traced to a mixture of these developments: the tax cut of 1964, increased government spending for domestic programs and the Vietnamese war, and the rapid growth of the money supply.

The Anatomy of Unemployment

Unemployment rates vary among particular groups of workers at specific moments in time as well as from year to year. Some types of persons are unemployed in recessions and some are unemployed even in the most prosperous years. The likelihood of being unemployed is not the same for all persons. As the figures in Table 2–3 show, in recession or in boom, teenagers, persons with limited skills and education, nonwhites, and construction workers have relatively high rates of unemployment.

The reasons for this concentration of unemployment are diverse. Teenagers are likely to be unemployed for some time when they enter the market to look for a first job and as they shift from job to job in search of one they like.

28

Table 2–2 UNEMPLOYMENT IN WESTERN ECONOMIES, 1959 TO 1969

Year	United States	Canada	Adjusted to U.S. concepts						As published					
			France	Germany (Federal Republic)	Great Britain	Italy	Japan	Sweden	France	Germany (Federal Republic)	Great Britain	Italy	Japan	Sweden
59	5.5	6.0	2.7	1.6	3.0	5.7	2.3		1.3	2.4	2.2	5.2	1.5	2.0
60	5.5	7.0	2.5	.8	2.0	4.3	1.7		1.3	1.2	1.6	4.0	1.1	1.4
61	6.7	7.1	1.9	.5	1.9	3.7	1.5	1.5	1.1	.8	1.5	3.4	1.0	1.2
62	5.5	5.9	1.8	.4	2.9	3.2	1.3	1.5	1.2	.7	2.0	3.0	.9	1.3
63	5.7	5.5	2.1	.5	3.5	2.7	1.3	1.7	1.4	.8	2.5	2.5	.9	1.4
64	5.2	4.7	1.6	.3	2.5	3.0	1.2	1.5	1.1	.7	1.6	2.7	.8	1.1
65	4.5	3.9	2.0	.3	2.2	4.0	1.2	1.2	1.4	.6	1.4	3.6	.8	1.1
66	3.8	3.6	2.1	.3	2.4	4.3	1.4	1.6	1.4	.7	1.5	3.9	.9	1.4
67	3.8	4.1	2.7	1.0	3.8	3.8	1.3	2.1	1.8	2.1	2.4	3.5	.9	1.7
68	3.6	4.8	3.2	1.2	3.7	3.8	1.2	2.2	2.1	1.5	2.4	3.5	1.2	2.2
69	3.5	4.7	2.8	.7	3.7	3.7	1.1	1.9	1.9	.8	2.4	3.4	1.1	1.9

Source: U.S. Department of Labor, Monthly Labor Review, Sept. 1970.

29

The minimum wage law, which requires the hourly rates of all workers, including inexperienced teenagers, to equal or to exceed a legally specified minimum may discourage employers from hiring and training young persons with limited job skills and experience. Some experts suggest exempting teenagers from the minimum wage law or establishing a lower minimum for them, as is common in Western Europe.

Relatively high unemployment of less-skilled and less-educated workers is probably related to the long-run decline in the demand for unskilled work which has outpaced the ability of these persons to acquire the training needed for higher-level jobs. In recessions, the unskilled are often laid off first because they are easily replaceable. Many jobs at the bottom of the barrel offer little opportunity for promotion or incentive for a permanent commitment to work.

Table 2–3   THE STRUCTURE OF UNEMPLOYMENT RATES IN TIGHT AND LOOSE LABOR MARKETS IN THE UNITED STATES

Group	Unemployment Rate		Change in Unemployment Rate
	Tight Labor Market (1968)	Loose Labor Market (1961)	1961–1968
All	3.6	6.7	−3.1
Men 20+	2.2		
White	2.0	5.1	−3.1
Nonwhite	3.9	11.7	−7.8
Women 20+	3.8	6.2	−2.4
White collar	2.0	3.8	−1.8
Craftsmen	2.4	6.3	−3.9
Operatives	4.5	9.6	−5.1
Laborers	7.2	14.5	−7.3
Teenagers 16–19			
Male	11.6	27.0	−16.4
Female	14.0	16.7	−2.7
Fifteen weeks or more of un- employment	0.5	2.1	−1.6
Construction	6.9	14.1	−7.2
Manufacturing	3.4	7.7	−4.3
Services and Finance	3.3	4.7	−1.4

The greater incidence of unemployment among nonwhites in the United States is due to several factors. Nonwhites are concentrated in jobs characterized by low skill and substantial unemployment. For example, nearly 20 percent of nonwhite males are laborers compared to about 5 percent of white males. Nonwhites also suffer from less education: in 1970 more than 57 percent of the nonwhite work force lacked a high school degree compared to just 35 percent of the white work force. Rough calculations suggest that from 40 to 60 percent of the difference between white and nonwhite unemployment rates is attributable to the unfavorable concentration of nonwhites at the bottom of the skill ladder. The remainder of the differential reflects many things, including discrimination in hiring and the location of many plants far from ghetto communities.

The seasonality of employment and the requisite changes in job sites explain the high unemployment in construction as workers move from one project to another and from one locale and employer to another.

Structural Unemployment and Manpower Policy

The existence of groups of individuals with relatively high unemployment rates even in prosperous times shows that not all nonfrictional unemployment is due to inadequate aggregate demand. At least some people are unemployed not because of a scarcity of jobs in the economy but because of a scarcity of the requisite skills. Either they lack the education or training to fill available vacancies or they live in communities such as coal towns or urban ghettos far removed from jobs. Unemployment arising from these factors is often called *structural unemployment*. Although a massive expansion in general demand might create such a great need for labor that the structurally unemployed would obtain employment, the cost in inflationary pressures would be extraordinary. A more effective method for reducing structural unemployment may be through an active "manpower policy" focusing on the particular problems of the unemployed. Among the elements of manpower programs, operating both on the quality of labor supply and on the demand for particular types of unemployed, are the following:

Training and retraining programs such as those initiated under the Manpower Development and Training Act

Improved elementary and secondary school education, especially vocational programs, for the disadvantaged

Work experience and training programs such as the Job Corps or Neighborhood Youth Corps

Improved labor-market information, perhaps through the use of the U.S. Employment Service and private employment agencies

Improved transportation for residents of urban ghettos

Greater enforcement of employment nondiscrimination laws

Assistance to depressed communities in the form of economic aid similar to the aid given less developed countries

Subsidies paid to private or public employers to pay for the incremental costs of hiring and training the disadvantaged

Selected Readings

Lewis, H. G., "Hours of Work and Hours of Leisure," in *Papers and Proceedings of the Ninth Annual Meeting*. Cleveland: Industrial Relations Research Association, 1956.

Manpower Report of the President, prepared annually by the United States Department of Labor.

Mincer, J., "Labor Force Participation," in *International Encyclopedia of Social Sciences*. New York: Macmillan, 1968.

———, "Labor Force Participation of Married Women," in Universities–NBER Committee, *Aspects of Labor Economics*. Princeton: Princeton University Press, 1962.

Ross, Arthur M., and Hill, Herbert, eds., *Employment, Race, and Poverty*. New York: Harcourt, Brace & Jovanovich, 1967.

Technology and the American Economy, Report of the National Commission on Technology, Automation, and Economic Progress, Vol. 1. Washington, D.C.: February, 1966.

Whyte, William F., *Money and Motivation, An Analysis of Incentives in Industry*. New York: Harper & Row, 1955.

Wolfbein, Seymour L., *Employment and Unemployment in the United States*. Chicago: Science Research Associates, Inc., 1964.

Education and Training

CHAPTER THREE

Mycologist, doffer, and offalman: these are some of the occupations currently found in the U.S. according to the Dictionary of Occupational Titles. The 21,000 occupations listed in the DOT differ in their degree of specialization, in the types of knowledge and physical skills required, in the wages paid, and in the places of employment. Some of the occupations are known to everyone; others, like those listed above, are known only to workers in these or in closely related positions.[1]

This chapter studies the changes in occupational and educational skills of the work force over time and the way in which workers acquire the numerous specialized job skills required for a modern economy.

LABOR-FORCE SKILLS AND ECONOMIC DEVELOPMENT

Economic development or industrialization is characterized by enormous shifts in the occupations and work skills of the labor force. The number of jobs requiring a high degree of skill and considerable

[1]They also are known to the compilers of the DOT, who define the occupations as follows:

Mycologist: performs research in the life processes of edible, poisonous, and parasitic fungi.

Doffer: removes bobbins of yarn from spindles of spinning or twisting frames in the textile industry.

Offalman: separates edible portions of butchered animals from waste parts in meat-packing plants.

33

educational preparation grows rapidly as a country industrializes, while the number of persons in unskilled jobs suffers a relative decline. Because industrialization involves the use of advanced technologies, the number of "high-level" workers—engineers, scientists, managers, professionals—increases especially rapidly.

The extent of the changed quality of the work force in the United States for the period from 1900 to 1969 is shown in Table 3–1. Jobs in agricultural activities and unskilled labor dropped from 50 percent to less than 10 percent of the work force during this period. The median number of years of schooling more than doubled. Following World War II, worker skills were upgraded at an accelerated pace. The number of professional and technical specialists burgeoned by more than 6 million and the number of farmers fell by 4+ million. Employment of scientists and engineers advanced many times more rapidly than total employment. A major transformation in the future of human work and of life in an industrial economy accompanied these trends.

Comparisons of worker skills in developed countries with those in less-developed countries tell a similar story. In a country such as Tanganyika for example, with a very low national product per person, there are fewer teachers, doctors, scientists, and engineers, and fewer persons attending school than in a wealthier country. In the most comprehensive study to date of the connection

Table 3–1 OCCUPATIONAL COMPOSITION OF THE AMERICAN WORK FORCE, 1900–1969

	Number of Persons (thousands)		Percentage Distribution of the Labor Force	
	1900	1969	1900	1969
Total Persons	29,030	77,487	100.0%	100.0%
White Collar	5,115	36,699	17.6	47.3
Professional, technical, and kindred	1,234	10,775	4.2	13.9
Managers, officials, and proprietors	1,697	7,985	5.8	10.3
Clerical and kindred	877	13,277	3.0	17.1
Sales	1,307	4,662	4.5	6.0
Manual and Service	13,027	37,341	44.8	48.1
Craftsmen, firemen, and kindred	3,062	10,020	10.5	12.9
Operatives	3,720	14,170	12.8	18.2
Laborers, except farm and mine	3,620	3,685	12.4	4.7
Service Workers	2,626	9,466	9.0	12.2
Farm Workers	10,888	3,447	37.5	4.4

Source: U.S. Bureau of the Census

Table 3–2   HUMAN RESOURCES IN DEVELOPED AND
LESS-DEVELOPED COUNTRIES

	United States	Italy	Yugoslavia	Tanganyika
GNP/capita	2577	516	265	61
Teachers/10,000 population	135	70	47	12
Engineers and scientists/ 10,000 pop.	62	35	22	½
Physicians and dentists/ 10,000 pop.	18	13	5	½
Pupils enrolled in school as percentage of 15–19-year-old population	95	35	16	2

Source: F. Harbison and C. A. Meyers, Education, Manpower & Economic Growth (New York: McGraw-Hill, 1964), Ch. 3, Tables 5–8.

between economic development and worker skills, professors Frederick Harbison (Princeton) and Charles Meyers (MIT) found levels of GNP per capita in 75 different countries associated with measures of "human resource development," as illustrated in Table 3–2.

The evidence for the United States and other countries over time and from many countries at one period of time is thus in agreement. Industrialization is accompanied by the development of a skilled and educated work force. Is this connection a necessary one? Why is economic growth characterized by human resource development?

Technology, Human Resources, and Economic Growth

An answer to these questions is found in the distinctive feature of modern economic growth—the application of scientific knowledge to the problems of production.

Consider the ways in which a society can obtain economic growth (increased output *per worker*). At any moment in time, the amount of goods and services that the work force can produce depends on the machines, equipment, and natural resources available, the work force's level of skill and efficiency, and on knowledge of what kinds of goods can be produced and how to produce them. Growth occurs when either (a) the number of machines and equipment (physical capital) increases, (b) additional natural resources are discovered, (c) the average level of skill or efficiency of workers increases, or (d) the stock of useful technological or social knowledge increases.

In the very long run, economic growth in advanced countries depends almost entirely on (d)—increases in the stock of knowledge. The addition of more physical capital with no change in technological knowledge can increase output for some time. Eventually, however, each added machine or piece of equipment will yield progressively smaller gains in productivity. Providing workers with more and more plows or oxen will never raise output to the level of modern developed economies. In a different way, the possibility of increasing output by the discovery of additional natural resources is also limited.[2] Educating or training people to produce goods in the best known way also runs into diminishing returns, for when the entire work force is fully educated or trained, all goods will be produced by "best practice" techniques and growth from education and training will end.

An advanced country, one with a large stock of capital, with fully utilized natural resources, and with a work force skilled and knowledgeable in modern production techniques, can thus grow only in one way. It must increase the amount of useful knowledge and apply this knowledge to production. The process of using new knowledge in economic activity to increase output is called *technological change*. A less-developed country can grow by adding to its stock of machines, by discovering and utilizing natural resources, or by introducing modern technology.

The connection between economic growth and changes in technology may partly explain the relationship between general economic development and human resource development. Economies which need improvements in technology to grow will demand "high-level" manpower capable of adding to the stock of knowledge, applying the knowledge to production, and teaching it to others. If they do not employ a great number of scientists, engineers, and other technically trained specialists, including managers and sales personnel, they will experience a decline in the rate of economic growth. Continual changes in technology will in turn alter the content of jobs and the skills, responsibilities, and tasks required of workers. Persons better able to adjust to continual change and learn new tasks will have an advantage in the labor market. As a result, education and training will be encouraged and human resources will be more fully developed than in other societies.

An Alternative View

The observed growth of education and skill among the production work force in a developing economy would have surprised the first students of industrialization. Karl Marx, you may recall, saw in the early industrialization of Western Europe a different future for modern economies. According to Marx, the workman

> becomes an appendage of the machine, and it is only the most simple, most monotonous, and most easily acquired knack, that is required of him. . . .[3]

[2] Perhaps in the future, when space travel permits us to use the natural resources of other planets, discovery of new supplies of resources will be a major source of growth!

[3] Capital, The Communist Manifesto, and other writings (N.Y., Modern Library, 1934), p. 328.

Machinery obliterates all distinctions of labour. . . .[4] In place of the hierarchy of specialized workmen . . . there steps, in the automatic factory, a tendency to equalize and reduce to one and the same level every kind of work.[5]

At the time Marx was writing, this was a plausible prediction. In the early stages of the Industrial Revolution, the need for some—though by no means all—types of skilled artisans declined noticeably. The demand for highly trained hand-loom weavers, for example, virtually disappeared as employers substituted power looms operated by unskilled women and children for these expensive specialists. Work in the new textile factories was often less pleasant and less skilled than the work previously performed in cottage industries. The necessity for factory discipline limited human freedoms.

Later stages of industrialization, however, failed to follow the initial tendency toward elimination of skilled work. It is difficult to say precisely why. From an engineering perspective, there is no reason for any particular technological changes to result in greater or less need for skilled workers. Even the most complex technologies in many cases are separable into a set of simple activities. Workers in a fully automated factory may need only a finger for button-punching. Perhaps the reason for the increased need for skilled workers is not solely derived from the *kind* of technology in industrial economics but from the speed with which technology *changes*. An educated and highly skilled work force is, as pointed out, likely to be better able to adjust to frequent changes in job tasks than a less-educated work force.

MARKETS FOR TRAINING AND EDUCATION

To explain past changes in worker skills or to predict future change, it is necessary to understand how the supply side of the market operates; how individuals choose an occupation and how institutions educate and train them.

Preparing someone for the world of work involves the operation of two different, though related markets—the labor market and the market for training and education. In the labor market, the demand for workers interacts with existing supply to determine wages and to allocate available workers among enterprises. In the market for training and education, individuals (who are suppliers in the labor market) demand training from a variety of training institutions—the formal educational system, private technical training schools,[6] employers with on-the-job training programs, and apprenticeship programs.

---

[4]*Op. cit.,* p. 330

[5]*Op. cit.,* p. 724

[6]One study reports 7000 private vocational schools with approximately 1.5 million students. A. Harvey Belitsky, *Private Vocational Schools and their Students* (Cambridge: Schenkman Publishing Co., 1969, p. 8.

37

Because the period for training or educating *high-level or skilled workers* is often long, the supply of specialists to a particular occupation may take some time to adjust to shifts in demand. The initial effect of an upward movement in demand for a given occupation will be to raise wages above the previous level. In the short run, there is likely to be very little change in supply. Some people with training in the specialty may enter from other occupations, whereas others, possibly women and older men, may decide to forgo leisure or retirement and remain at work. For the most part, though, supply is inelastic. As time proceeds, however, the higher wages increase the attractiveness of a skilled occupation. Young persons originally considering different careers will be drawn into the occupation by the new wage level and employment opportunities and seek the requisite training. As long as the facilities for training are flexible, the number of trainees and eventually the number of new specialists will grow, shifting the supply schedule to the right. In the short run supply is inelastic; in the long run, it responds to economic incentives.[7]

Additional understanding of the adjustment of supply to changed conditions requires a more detailed look at career decisions and at the institutions that train persons for the world of work.

Career Choice and Investment in Human Capital

Occupational choice depends on both economic and noneconomic factors. To isolate the effect of economic variables, the economist usually assumes that noneconomic phenomena, such as preferences or abilities, are relatively fixed in a population; he therefore focuses on the relation between changes in economic conditions and behavior.

The most important economic variable in career decision is wages or salaries. In evaluating the economic worth of an occupation, the individual will estimate the prospective salary he is likely to earn and the cost of training for the occupation. The individual will take account of the earnings possibilities over his entire working life, *discounted* at a suitable rate of interest, relative to earnings elsewhere in the market.

Earnings over one's entire working life must be considered because the salaries offered by different occupations vary with age. Engineers, for instance, receive relatively high starting salaries but obtain relatively small increments to salary with age (see Fig. 3–1). Business executives, on the other hand, initially earn a lower salary than engineers, but enjoy more rapid increases with age. To make a rational evaluation of the relative monetary advantages of these occupations, one must look at the entire "age–earnings curve."

[7]What do we mean by *long run* and *short run*? It depends on the number of years required to train a new man. For a college-trained Bachelor of Science in engineering, for instance, training takes 4 to 5 years. For a computer programmer with very limited skills, 4 to 5 months may suffice. For a mathematical specialist in programming, a Ph.D. degree might be needed.

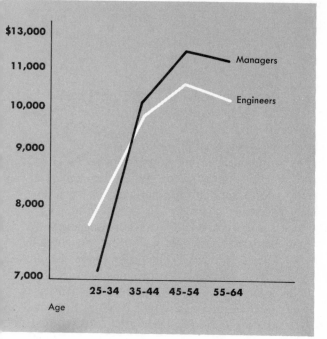

FIG. 3–1 Median earnings over the life cycle in engineering and management, for males. *Source:* U.S. Census of Population, 1959.

"Discounting to present value" enters the economic calculation because of the need to compare dollars received today with dollars to be received in the future. With a positive market rate of interest, a dollar today will be worth more than a dollar one year from now. This is because a dollar today can always be invested at the current interest rate and grow to more than a dollar next year. At 5 percent interest, you can invest a dollar today and have $1.05 next year. Similarly, to receive a dollar next year, all you need this year is $1/$1.05, or 95¢. Hence, next year's dollar, discounted to its present value, is worth 95¢ today. Dollars received one year apart differ in value by 5 percent because the market rate of interest is 5 percent.

What about $1 received N years in the future? The present value of this dollar can be found by the same line of reasoning. We simply calculate the amount of money which, invested today at 5 percent, is worth $1 N years in the future. At 5 percent compound interest, a dollar invested today is worth $($1.05$)^N$ dollars N years from now. Thus the present value of $1 payable in N years is $$1.00/(1.05)^N$.

The present value of money to be received in the future declines rapidly as the number of years (N) increases with the 5 percent of interest. A dollar payable two years from now is worth about 91¢; one payable ten years from now is valued at 61¢ and one 25 years in the future has a present value of 30¢.

To compute the "discounted lifetime income" in an occupation, we take the income received at each year in the working life, discount it to the present, and sum up all of the discounted incomes. The formula for this computation is

$$PV = \frac{Y_1}{(1+r)} + \frac{Y_2}{(1+r)^2} + \ldots + \frac{Yn}{(1+r)n}$$

where PV is the present value, Y_1 the income received in Year 1, Y_2 the income in Year 2, and so on; r represents the rate of interest. In this case, the individual works for n years and then presumably retires.

Estimates of discounted present values of lifetime incomes for men at age 18 in 1966 for different levels of education are summarized in Table 3–3. The table uses several interest rates to compute present values. Economists are undecided about the appropriate rate to apply to lifetime incomes. Some favor a 4 to 5 percent rate, which is roughly equal to the return from government bonds or from money in a savings account. Others have suggested that the average rate of return on corporate manufacturing investment, estimated by Professor George Stigler to be about 7 percent, is the appropriate discount factor.[8] If we are considering a student who must borrow money at bank or credit loan rates, the rate could be much higher—8 to 18 percent. The particular rate chosen affects the pattern of lifetime incomes. Notice that in Table 3–3 the income of educated workers exceeds that of less-educated workers at the lower rates of interest. At the highest rates, the educated men do worse. Why is this?

The reason is simple. A person going to college or engaging in similar training or education programs gives up four (or more) years of work and thus loses four years of income compared to someone who enters the labor force directly. This sacrifice of income which could have been earned had the student gone to work represents the *foregone earnings* of schooling. It is the hidden cost of schooling—that part due not to direct spending on tuition or books but to the opportunities given up in order to attend school.[9]

The educated person forgoes earnings in the present because his education "pays off" in the future. He expects to earn more in the future than the less-educated individual. But dollars received in the future are worth less than present dollars. Indeed, at a very high rate of interest, future dollars will be worth relatively little—at 20 percent a dollar received seven years in the future is worth only 23¢. Hence, at high rates of interest, the educated man who gives up

---

[8]Stigler, *Capital and Rates of Return in Manufacturing Industries*, National Bureau of Economic Research (Princeton: Princeton University Press, 1963).

[9]What proportion of the total cost of schooling is accounted for by foregone earnings? About 60 percent, according to estimates by T. W. Schultz and others. Does this seem to be too much? Think of the student who attends a free state university or receives a scholarship. His direct costs of schooling—the cost of books, library fines, and such are very small compared to the income foregone from work.

Table 3–3 PRESENT VALUES OF LIFETIME INCOMES FOR MALES AT
AGE 18 IN 1966

Years of School Completed	Expected Lifetime Income with Discount rate of		
	0%	5%	20%
College 4 or more years	$760,000	$260,000	24,000
College 1–3 years	585,000	171,000	23,000
High school 4 years	508,000	154,000	28,000
High school 1–3 years	428,000	129,000	22,400
Elementary school, 8 years	373,000	120,000	32,000
Elementary school, less than 8 years	282,000	93,000	20,000

Source: Calculated from Figures in U.S. Department of Commerce, Consumer Income, Series
P-60 No. 56. Commerce figures are adjusted in several ways: (1) for the direct cost of schooling;
(2) for income by persons with less than a high-school education prior to age 18; (3) alternative
fourth the income of those in the school category directly below them; (4) incomes extrapolated
estimates of income during school were made under the assumption that persons make one-
into the future under the assumption that all incomes increase at 2 percent per annum.

present income to receive income later in life will have a lower present value of
discounted income than the less educated man, who earns money now. Conversely, at low rates of interest, money in the future is worth almost as much as
money today and the educated man does better in terms of present value than
the less educated.

The decision to forgo present income and pay tuition expenses to attend
school or to undergo training can be looked upon as an *investment in human
capital*. The cost of the investment is the sum of all direct expenses such as
tuition for schooling and foregone earnings. The return on the investment is the
increased earnings brought about by education or training.

Viewed in this manner, the rate of return or profitability of investing in
human capital can be compared to the returns from investing in other kinds of
projects. How does the return on investing in high-school and college education
compare to other investments?

Gary Becker, Professor of Economics at The University of Chicago, has
attempted to answer this question. Becker calculated the rate of return from
college and high-school education in the same way that the businessman calcu-
lates the rate of return on business investment. He finds that investing in high-
school and college education is profitable, on average. The rate of return
to a white male for spending four years in high school in 1958 was, according to his figures, 28 percent. The return on a college education was in
the area of 15 percent. The higher rate for high school is due partly to the
higher incomes foregone by college men as compared to high school men and
to the high unemployment rate among men without a high-school diploma,
which makes the foregone income of high school relatively small.

41

For other people in society, white women and nonwhites, the return on education appears to be smaller. However, these rates are still above those received from many other kinds of investment. An investment in a college education, even ignoring the pleasures of school and the "noneconomic" benefits of education, is a good investment decision.

The choice of an occupation depends on expectations of the future, but unless you possess psychic powers, there is no guarantee that your anticipations of income levels or working conditions will be fulfilled. Investment in human capital, like investment in physical plant or in the stock market, is a risky and uncertain proposition.

Two factors underlie the risk and uncertainty of occupational choice. First is the possibility that the state of the market for an entire profession may alter in an unexpected way. Improvements in computer technology might, for example, reduce the need for programmers or mathematicians. If this occurs, the salaries and jobs in these fields will decline contrary to the expectations of the thousands of persons seeking programming or mathematical training today. Similarly, changes in the demand for labor in different industries or activities may completely reorient a labor market. A case in point is the curtailment in federal expenditures for the space program in the late 1960's and early 1970's, which drastically reduced demand for engineers, physicists, and other space-age specialists. In the span of a few years public concern over possible "shortages" of scientific specialists changed into concern about unemployed engineers or about Ph.D. and M.S. scientists forced into nonscientific jobs.

A second reason for riskiness in career choice is that an individual cannot be sure of his own success or failure in a given area of work. Indeed, at any time the income received by workers in an occupation varies considerably around the average income (Fig. 3–2.). No one necessarily receives the average. In some cases such as the legal profession, the variation of income is extremely high, indicating that the law student can only be loosely guided by the average income in legal work. In other careers, such as teaching, the variation is much smaller. Although the individual choosing a career undoubtedly has some idea about where he stands in comparison to other people, eventual economic success is not assured. The one way in which he can minimize the risk of his investment is to select a career in which the dispersion of income is especially small.

Nonmonetary Factors and the Marginal Decision Maker

A moment's introspection tells us that the choice of career depends on much more than monetary factors. The kind of work we like (or dislike the least), our ability to perform different tasks, special contacts and access, as well as accidents and choice all play a role in the occupational decision.

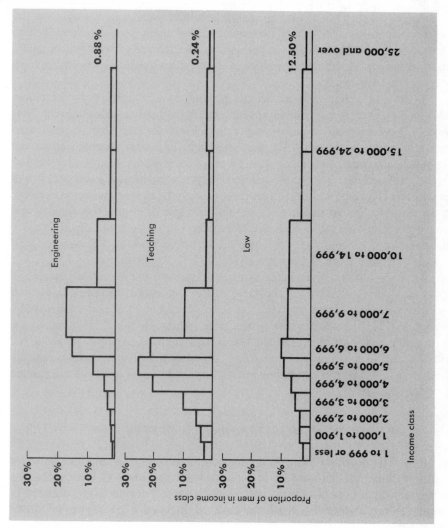

FIG. 3–2 Variations of income for males aged 25 to 64 in law, teaching, and engineering.
Source: U.S. Census of Population, 1959.

Because of nonmonetary preferences and differential abilities, the career decisions of most persons are unaffected by an increase in wages in a particular occupation (relative to wages elsewhere). Those with great love for certain types of work, for instance priests and ministers, choose that work at almost any "reasonable" wage. Others with specialized abilities will select a career on the basis of their particular "ability endowment." For these people money income is not the principal aspect of a job relevant to their choice or even an especially important aspect. Moderate wage changes in the labor market will probably have no impact on their behavior.

At the same time, however, some persons have abilities and preferences which make several occupations appear equally attractive under current conditions. These *marginal decision makers* are likely to alter their career plans when relative wages change. All else remaining the same, they will select the occupation enjoying the greatest gain in income. If many people are "on the margin" between careers, supply will be highly elastic; if only a few are, it will be inelastic. The responsiveness of the labor supply to changes in wages depends on the possibly limited number of persons to whom the other advantages and disadvantages of alternative occupations balance out. It does not depend on the existence of a mythical species of *homo oeconomicus* who like Scrooge McDuck view life strictly in terms of the almighty dollar.

Table 3–4 summarizes some evidence regarding the actual adjustment of supply to changes in salaries. The table relates percentage increases in median doctorate salaries, which presumably influence the selection of a specialty, to the number of Ph.D. graduates five years later. Although the correlation is not perfect, there is a definite positive association between changes in economic incentive and in the supply of specialists. Investment in human capital appears to respond to economic conditions in this market in accord with the economic theory of supply.

INSTITUTIONS FOR TRAINING WORKERS

The decisions to invest in education and training create a demand for training facilities. If the number of newly trained specialists is to increase, the supply of training opportunities must respond to the demand. The number of openings in medical schools must, for instance, increase if the supply of M.D.'s is to increase.

In an industrial economy a number of institutions are involved in the training process: the formal educational system, private technical training schools and programs such as secretarial schools and correspondence courses, the formal apprenticeship system, formal or informal on-the-job training programs, and special government training programs. Different economies place different emphasis on each of these mechanisms. In the United States the edu-

Table 3–4 SUPPLY ADJUSTMENTS TO CHANGES IN SALARIES IN THE
DOCTORATE LABOR MARKET

Doctorate Specialty	Percentage change in salary, 1948–57	Percentage change in graduates, 1953 & 1954— 1962 & 1963	Rank order by change in salary/degree	
Pathology	98.9	187.5	1	2
Mechanical Engineering	81.7	122.0	2	4
Electrical Engineering	78.7	180.2	3	3
Inorganic Chemistry	78.6	52.9	4	12
Chemical Engineering	65.8	65.4	5	8
Analytical Chemistry	65.0	67.0	6	7
Physics	61.3	47.4	7	16
Mathematics	61.1	88.1	8	5
Physical Chemistry	60.8	37.4	9	18
Aeronautical Engineering	58.3	72.2	10	6
Organic Chemistry	52.9	32.8	11	20
Civil Engineering	51.7	274.7	12	1
Metallurgical Engineering	49.8	57.8	13	11
Geology	49.6	57.4	14	10
Entomology	46.0	48.7	15	15
Pharmacology	45.0	32.4	16	21
Anatomy	44.1	40.3	17	17
Zoology	43.6	9.7	18	23
Physiology	43.1	2.2	19	24
Microbiology	41.6	50.6	20	14
Astronomy	41.4	60.6	21	9
Biochemistry	40.6	52.2	22	13
Agriculture	39.8	−7.5	23	26
Psychology	39.3	35.2	24	19
Botany	36.2	−6.3	25	25
Geography	35.3	32.2	26	22

Source: R.B. Freeman, *The Market for College-Trained Manpower* (Cambridge, Mass.: Harvard University Press, 1971), Chap. 7.

cational system and on-the-job training appear to be the most important ways of training workers. In recent years, the role of private vocational schools in training persons for specific occupations has increased, with large firms entering the field. In many European countries, on the other hand, apprenticeship is a more important training mechanism than in the United States.

The Formal School System

The school system—elementary and secondary schools and institutions of higher learning—can be viewed as an industry "selling education" to students and their parents. As an industry, the school system differs from ordinary industries. Schools are primarily nonprofit organizations; many of the costs of schooling are financed by endowments or governmental subsidies. These differences

45

should not, however, disguise the role of schools as producers of human capital analogous to that of machinery manufacturing companies as producers of physical capital.

Many Americans are trained for their occupations in postsecondary schools—colleges, technical institutes, schools of accounting, universities, law schools, and so on. Although most schools are not subject to the discipline of the market in the same way as profit-making firms, the courses offered reflect the demand for training by students. Increased desire for training in mathematics, for example, has produced substantial increases in the number of schools offering graduate programs in the field and in the employment of mathematicians and university faculty. Similarly, the demand for urban studies, black or Afro-American studies, or biochemistry causes the educational system to alter the course offerings. One of the most dramatic effects of the demand for training on educational institutions can be seen in the growing number of computer-programming schools. Ten or fifteen years ago there were virtually no programming schools; today you find advertisements from institutions specializing in programming in nearly every large newspaper and in many matchbooks.

The Apprenticeship System

Apprenticeship offers a mixture of on-the-job and formal classroom training that dates back to the guilds of the Middle Ages. It is the dominant method of training for certain craftsmen, such as electricians, plumbers and pipefitters, sheetmetal workers, and in some of the printing trades. In other crafts, including painting and cooking, most workers acquire skills in less formal and systematic ways. The apprentice works at the various aspects of his job and takes related classroom work for a period of three to five years. Many programs provide for 1200 to 1600 hours of related classroom instruction—as many as college students take in a normal four-year program. The wage of the apprentice increases each six months or year until the journeyman rate is achieved.

Apprenticeship programs are under the direction of joint labor–management committees, or of employers alone in unorganized sectors, who establish the apprenticeship standards, prescribe the training, and arrange for the financing of the program. One of the most extensive national programs is that for the plumbing and pipefitting crafts. Each year, in connection with the national apprenticeship contest, instructors in the program are brought to Purdue University for a week of courses on new developments and technological changes in the trade. In August, 1970, more than 1100 instructors participated in these courses financed by the industry and administered by a joint labor–management committee. A number of apprenticeship programs have been expanded to include journeyman training, providing instruction on new developments in certain crafts to journeymen who received their training years ago. The instruction in new methods of welding and welding with new alloys in the plumbing and pipefitting program is an illustration.

One of the most significant questions related to occupational training concerns the range of tasks included in the program. The more narrow and limited the set of tasks, the shorter the program and the smaller the costs. Workers trained in this way, however, may suffer from problems of obsolescence and unemployment in unstable labor markets. As a result, workers and labor unions often prefer a broad range of training which serves as insurance against both technological displacement and cyclical ups and downs. Under various economic conditions an operating engineer who has experience operating a back hoe, a bulldozer, and a crane, for example, may expect more work than one who can operate only a single machine. Employers, however, may well prefer to reduce the costs of training by more specialization and to divide broad craft jobs into specialized tasks with lower wage rates for each. The resolution of these differences is one task of collective bargaining; negotiations compel each side to consider their long-run interests and to recognize that training policy is partly dependent on stability of employment.

On-the-Job Training

Because it often occurs in an informal setting, on-the-job training is the most difficult training institution to evaluate. One worker in a factory shows another how to perform some task; a worker assists another and picks up some knowledge about the other man's job. One worker is sick or on vacation and the rules of the internal labor market specify that another will gain some experience on the absent worker's job. The extent of such informal education can scarcely be estimated directly. Nonetheless, it seems that on-the-job training in industry is one of the principal ways of teaching vocational skills to workers. Surveys of *formal* training programs in private industry, for instance, indicate that firms spend a considerable amount on training. In New England, seven of every ten manufacturing firms have industrial training programs. Almost one-fifth of New England's manufacturing labor force receives training each year. For this purpose, manufacturers spend more than $70 million a year. This is one-eighth as much as their annual outlay for new plant and equipment.[10]

Indirect estimates of the total amount of formal and informal on-the-job training in the United States by Professor Jacob Mincer provide additional evidence of the importance of this training mechanism. According to Mincer, "measured in terms of costs, [on-the-job training] is as important as formal education for the male labor force.[11]

Just as with formal education in the school system, training in the firm generally has a characteristic line of advancement. This is the skill or promo-

---

[10]"Industrial Investment in Manpower," *New England Business Review* (February, 1964), including technical supplement.

[11]"On-the-Job Training: Costs, Returns, and Some Implications," *Journal of Political Economy, Supplement* (October, 1962).

tion ladder of the internal labor market. An unskilled worker who enters the factory will be hired at an "entry port" for the bottom job in a given skill ladder. As he accumulates seniority and obtains greater skills, he will be promoted "up the ladder." Each job on the ladder is closely related to ones surrounding it so that informal training often suffices to teach workers the skills needed for upward mobility. In the steel industry, for example, a worker may rise inside the bargaining unit from the lowest rung, Job Class 1–2, to the highest-paid Job Class 32. A worker choosing a job among factories or selecting a "ladder" within a firm would presumably select the one with, *ceteris paribus*, the greatest present value of discounted lifetime income.

It is often useful to distinguish between two types of on-the-job training: *general* training which, like formal education, prepares a person to work for any of a number of employers; and *specific* training, which is useful only at the current place of work. An example of the former is the training needed to be an electrician; an example of the latter is the training needed to handle the electrical problems of the Chicago plant of Jones Manufacturing. The division of the economic benefits and costs of training between employers and employees differs greatly in the two cases. General training will never be financed by employers, since workers can always quit after being trained and use the training in competitive establishments. The cost of investing in general on-the-job training and the economic return from such investments will, like the benefits and costs of formal schooling, be limited to the individual.

When training is specific to a firm, the situation is different. In this case the firm need not worry about employees using the training elsewhere. They will be willing to invest in specific training with the intention of obtaining benefits in the form of more productive workers. Analogously, workers will be willing to make such investments if they obtain some of the return. Both employers and employees will share in the cost of investing and in the returns of specific training. After the training is complete, when employers and employees are earning "profits" from the investment, they will be especially valuable to each other. Firms will be relatively unwilling to lay off or fire workers in which they have made large investments; employees will be relatively unwilling to quit jobs in which they have made investments and are earning returns.

Government Training Programs

In recent years special government training programs have been initiated as part of "active manpower policy." Both in Europe and in North America, governments either train or finance the training of many unskilled persons, the technologically displaced, and regional migrants. In addition the governments support, through scholarship policies and direct aid to educational institutions, the education of postsecondary-school students. In its policies toward the draft and the procurement of military manpower, the government also has a significant impact on the quality of the labor force.

In 1960 the United States federal expenditure on manpower programs was approximately $250 million; a decade later expenditures were over $3 billion a year, more than a tenfold increase. The legislative cornerstone of this expansion is the Manpower Development and Training Act of 1962 and its subsequent amendments. The initial thrust of the legislation was to provide institutional or classroom training and on-the-job occupational and skill training for those unemployed through technological displacement and regional shifts of industry (coal miners in Appalachia and textile workers in New England). As the decade of the 1960's progressed and high levels of employment were achieved in the economy, the center of concern shifted to manpower programs for the economically disadvantaged and racial minorities. A variety of programs were developed for youth, older workers, low-skilled workers in need of upgrading in training, those with medical problems, those seeking new careers in subprofessional occupations and service industries, those on welfare, and so on. In varying degrees these programs provided a wide range of services including recruitment, counseling, testing, placement, orientation, remedial and skill training and related instruction, job development in private and public employment, residential training centers, and basic education. These programs involve in varying degrees community action groups, civil rights groups, local and state government agencies, labor organizations, and private employers.

As the volume of expenditures rose and the diversity of programs and agencies multiplied in the 1960's, it became apparent that a greater degree of coordination and leadership was essential.[12] The Manpower Administration in the Department of Labor was established and made a more effective agency. Local planning agencies (Cooperative Area Manpower Planning System— CAMPS) were established to bring together various state, local, and federal agencies in metropolitan and local areas. In the United States, a comprehensive manpower program for the disadvantaged is still very much in the developmental stage at the outset of the 1970's. The mix of private and public agencies is in doubt; the coordination of federal, state, and local agencies leaves much to be desired; the state of the art of manpower projection and planning is rudimentary.

It is difficult to assess the relative costs and benefits of government manpower programs. It is clear that a high level of aggregate demand and a low level of general unemployment is essential to the success of any governmental training program. But it is difficult to know which persons have a job only because of a government program, or to predict what would have happened in the absence of these programs. The rate of turnover of persons classified as disadvantaged is high, and relatively low-paid jobs without obvious career opportunities are widely available in the labor market without significant training or education. The transformation of jobs and the change in public and private

employment practices to attract, train, and retain the disadvantaged is still to
be generally achieved.

Like gypsy fortune-tellers, economists and policy makers try to predict the
future. The important role of trained manpower in growth and the startling
shifts in the demand for workers produced by economic change place a
premium on accurate predictions of future manpower needs.

The advantages of accurate predictions to individuals choosing their
occupations, to firms, to educational institutions, and to governments are
numerous. Advance information about shifts in the demand for labor reduces
the risk of investing in human capital. Persons choosing an occupation and
guidance counselors advising them make wiser decisions. Firms and government
agencies are able to evaluate the feasibility of launching new programs requiring
skilled workers. Educational and training programs can be initiated today so
that the future supply of manpower "meshes" with future demand. The dual
dangers of "shortages" of skilled workers creating bottlenecks in economic
growth and "surpluses" of workers with outmoded skills are avoided. Accurate
forecasts can help reduce the period of adjustment in the labor market and in
the market for training and education.

The nature of investing in human capital dictates that forecasts and planning be long term. This is because the time span between the initiation of education or training and the production of trained workers is lengthy. If significant
changes in the supply of training facilities—school buildings and teachers—
are needed, the time lag between the formulation of plans and their realization
can be perhaps ten or more years. New medical schools with construction
started in 1970 will not produce finished medical specialists for a decade.

Current methods of manpower forecasting are relatively primitive. The
most frequently used technique, the "manpower requirements approach," is
based on drastically simplified assumptions about the operation of the labor
market, which amount to simply extrapolating past and present conditions of
employment.

The simplest type of requirements analysis assumes that the number of
skilled workers employed in *particular industries* is the correct number or has
been growing at the correct rate. Then, on the basis of forecasts of the demand
for the products of the various industries and of the accompanying growth of
total employment, the needs for workers in particular categories in the future
are estimated. The method thus focuses on the *effect of differences in the growth
of industries* on demand for workers, ignoring the possibility that changes in
technology may drastically alter the demand for particular categories of workers

[12]See Stanley H. Ruttenberg, Manpower Challenge of the 1970's: Institutions and Social Change
(Baltimore: Johns Hopkins, 1970).

in all industries and the possibility that past employment was not at the correct level.

Sophisticated manpower requirements forecasters such as the United States Bureau of Labor Statistics attempt to adjust for the simplifications of the method. The BLS describes its methods for projecting in 1963 the requirements for scientists, engineers and technicians to 1970 as follows:[13]

(1) Ratios of scientists and engineers to total employment were established for each sector of the civilian economy—including private industry, government, and college and universities—for the base year 1960—and for all previous years for which data were available.

(2) Trends in the ratios were projected to 1970.

(3) The projected ratios for each industry were then applied to *independent* 1970 projections of total employment by industry to yield first approximations of scientific and engineering manpower requirements in 1970. (The total employment projections were derived from a study of the future growth of demand for the goods of different industries and of changes in productivity.)

(4) The first approximations of 1970 scientific and engineering manpower requirements developed in (3) were then examined in detail and analyzed for reasonableness.

What is perhaps most striking about this technique is the complete absence of any reference to wages and salaries. In projecting the future course of the labor market, wage as well as quantity information should be of use. Wages, after all, are an important determinant of the supply of workers to different occupations and of the employment decisions of firms. When wages (or rates of return) differ greatly among occupational fields, it is safe to expect differential rates of growth in the number of persons choosing them. When shifts in the mix of industries raise demand for some occupations and reduce it for others, changes in wages (increases in the former case, decreases in the latter) can be expected to ameliorate the effect on employment.

[13]Bureau of Labor Statistics, Long-Range Demand for Scientists and Technical Personnel—A Methodological Study (NSF 61—65, 1961)

Selected Readings

Becker, G. S., *Human Capital*. New York: Columbia University Press, 1964.

Blau, Peter M., and Duncan, Otis Dudley, *The American Occupational Structure*. New York: John Wiley, 1964.

Bowen, William G., *Economic Aspects of Education, Three Essays*. Princeton, N. J.: Industrial Relations Section, Princeton University, 1964.

Denison, Edward F., *Why Growth Rates Differ, Postwar Experience in Nine Western Countries*. Washington, D.C.: The Brookings Institution, 1967.

Freeman, Richard B., *The Market for College-Trained Manpower*. Cambridge, Mass.: Harvard University Press, 1971.

Harbison, Frederick, and Myers, Charles A., *Education, Manpower and Economic Growth*. New York: McGraw-Hill, 1964.

Mangum, Garth L., *MDTA: Foundation of Federal Manpower Policy*. Baltimore: Johns Hopkins, 1968.

Nelson, R. R.; Peck, M. S.; and Kalachek, E. O., *Technology, Economic Growth, and Public Policy*. Washington, D.C.: The Brookings Institution, 1969, chapters 1, 2, and 6.

Schultz, Theodore W., *The Economic Value of Education*. New York: Columbia University Press, 1963.

——, *Investment in Human Capital*. New York: The Free Press, 1971.

The Demand for Labor

CHAPTER FOUR

WORKERS IN JAPAN
ARE SOUGHT AFTER

**One Manufacturer in
Tokyo Resorts to
Kidnapping**

TOKYO—Losing a valuable employe to a rival company was too much for Yohiro Ishihara, operator of a leather goods concern.

Mr. Ishihara, 48 years old, rounded up eight of his workers, including his son, and abducted Yoshihiro Sato, the former employe, from his home. They took him to a seaside shack and threatened him until Mr. Sato agreed to return to the company. To make sure that Mr. Sato would not change his mind, they tied him up and left him in the shack for the night.

Although the demand for labor rarely takes the extreme form of midnight kidnappings, the need for workers, especially those with high skills, is considerable in a healthy economy. What determines the level of demand in different firms, industries, or countries? How are workers allocated among employers under ordinary circumstances? What causes changes in demand?

THE ANALYSIS OF LABOR DEMAND

The demand for labor is different from that for commodities. In the first place, employers do not hire labor for the intrinsic pleasure of having employees, the way consumers purchase goods or services.[1] Workers are hired because they help produce goods for consumers, investors, or other firms. This means that the demand for labor is a *derived* demand, dependent on the demand for goods. Whenever the demand for goods changes, all else being equal, the demand for labor changes in the same direction. An increase or decrease in the demand for houses, for instance (brought about perhaps by changed mortgage rates) will increase or decrease the demand for plumbers, carpenters, masons, and other construction workers. Furthermore, employers rarely want only to hire workers. For the most part, modern production requires the simultaneous usage of several inputs—labor, machinery and materials. To produce an automobile, for instance, calls for workers *and* machinery *and* steel, rubber, aluminum, and so on. Thus the demand for labor is part of a joint demand for labor and other factors of production. Under some circumstances, the number and kind of workers required by a firm depends critically on the availability of other factors —such as the machines in use. A large crane, for instance, needs one man to run it; demand for operators is therefore part and parcel of the number of cranes in use and the demand for additional cranes.

The variables which determine the number of workers desired in an enterprise, industry, or economy are usually examined in two stages: Stage one concentrates on the relation between the wage rate and the number of workers demanded, with other variables, especially the demand for goods, held fixed. The association between wages and quantity demanded is called the *demand curve for labor*. Like other demand curves, it is downward sloping: increases in wages reduce the employment of workers, all else remaining the same. The quantitative size of the change in employment is measured by the *elasticity* of the curve, the percentage change in employment due to a one percent change in wages.[2] The significance of a particular change in wages depends on the elasticity of demand. With a very elastic curve, a 10 percent wage change might

---

[1]The pretty secretary, the newly appointed vice-president whose father owns the company, or the employer who discriminates in employment are exceptions to this general rule.

[2]Let Q = number of workers demanded and w = the wage rate. Then the elasticity is % change in Q/% change in w.

produce an enormous decline in employment; with an inelastic curve, virtually no one is displaced.

In the second stage of analysis, the factors that shift the demand curve by increasing or decreasing the number desired at fixed wage rates are the subject of study. The most important of the demand-shift variables are changes in the demand for commodities and changes in the technology of production.

This chapter examines the decision to hire labor, the determinants of the elasticity of demand, and the main factors shifting the curve. We investigate the demand in a single firm first, then in a particular market, and finally in the entire economy.

The Firm's Demand for Labor

Consider an employer who is deciding whether to hire an additional worker. At the moment, 600 men work in his factory. Shall he increase the work force to 601 (or, possibly, reduce it to 599 or some other number)? If the employer wants to *maximize profits*, how might he go about reaching the employment decision?

First the employer will estimate the change in output in the factory resulting from the employment of another worker. This change in output is called the *marginal physical product of labor* (MPP_L).

Second, the employer will calculate the amount of money he is likely to receive as a result of the sale of the increase in output. If there is a "going price" in the product market, the amount received equals the added output multiplied by the price of the product: $MPP_L \cdot P$.[3] This multiplicand ($MPP_L \cdot P$) is the value of the marginal product of labor. It represents the additional dollars received from the prospective increase in employment.

The final step in the decision is to compare $MPP_L \cdot P$ with the cost of hiring the worker. In a perfectly competitive labor market, this cost is just "the going wage rate" (W) as the employer is presumably able to hire the desired number of workers at the going rate. If the wage is below the value of labor's marginal contribution to output, the employer will increase the work force; if it is greater than $MPP_L \cdot P$, he decreases the work force. Whenever the cost of hiring (which may include recruitment expenses beyond wage rates) differs from the dollars added by an additional worker, the employer will be dissatisfied with present employment. By changing the number of employees, he can increase profits. Only when $MPP_L \cdot P = W$ will the profit-maximizing employer be satisfied with the level of employment in his firm. The equality of the value of labor's marginal product and the cost of labor is the *equilibrium* condition for employment. If employment is initially in equilibrium and the wage increases, the employer will lay off some men; if the wage increases, he will hire additional workers. Figure 4–1 depicts graphically the equilibrium level of employment

[3] If the employer is so large that the price depends on his output, the amount of money obtained from an increase is $MPP_L \cdot MR$ where MR = marginal revenue from additional sales.

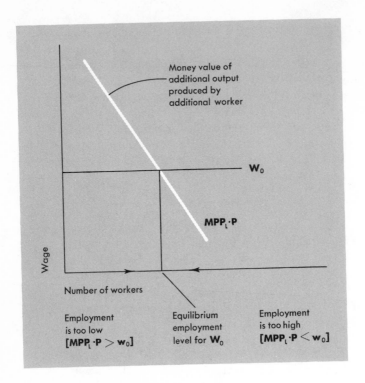

Money value of
additional output
produced by
additional worker

W_0

$MPP_L \cdot P$

Wage

Number of workers

Employment is too low	Equilibrium employment level for W_0	Employment is too high
$[MPP_L \cdot P > w_0]$		$[MPP_L \cdot P < w_0]$

FIG. 4–1 Determination of employment.

to a firm and shows the direction of change when the equilibrium is not satisfied.

The reason for the inverse relation between wages and the equilibrium level of employment lies in the technology of production. Under any given technology the marginal product of labor declines as the number of employees increases. This is the famous *law of diminishing returns* which, formally stated, reads:

> As the amount of any one factor is increased, the amounts of all other factors remaining fixed, the marginal product of the factor that varies will fall.[4]

The idea behind diminishing returns is straightforward: with a fixed amount of machinery and materials, increases in employment reduce the machinery and materials avaliable to each worker and thus lower the advantage of additional workers. The decline in MPP_L as employment grows and conversely the increase in MPP_L as employment falls tell us the *direction* of change needed to restore equilibrium.

Take, for instance, the case of an increase in wages. Prior to the increase, the employer will have hired just enough workers to make the value of the marginal product of labor equal the cost of labor:

56

[4]R. Dorfman, *Price and Markets* (Englewood Cliffs, N. J.: Prentice-Hall, 1967), p. 69.

$$MPP_L \, (L, \overline{K}) \cdot \overline{P} = \overline{W}$$

where the bars above the symbols denote those quantities which are determined by forces beyond the employer's immediate control. P and W are set by the going wage or price in the market whereas the amount of capital (K) is set by previous decisions by the employer.

The increase in wage disturbs the equality by making W greater, *at the margin*, than the money received from employing L workers. To restore the equality, the employer must change L so that the value of labor's marginal product $(MPP_L \, (L, \overline{K}) \cdot \overline{P})$ increases But, according to the law of diminishing returns, only a reduction in employment will raise MPP_L. Accordingly, the firm lowers employment until the increase in $MPP_L \, (L, \overline{K}) \cdot \overline{P}$ just suffices to make employment once again profitable at the margin.

The downward slope in the demand for labor is thus explicable in terms of the marginal product of labor and diminishing returns to labor when other factors are fixed. This is one statement of the *marginal productivity theory of demand*.

The Firm's Demand When Other Inputs Vary

You will notice that our analysis of the employment decision has assumed that labor is the only input which can be varied in response to the change in wages. For short periods of time, this is a reasonable assumption, particularly when the other primary inputs are capital goods—machinery, equipment, and buildings—which last a long time and cannot be immediately replaced. As time proceeds, however, the firm can change its employment of nonlabor resources as well as its employment of labor. With higher labor costs due to increased wages, will firms be satisfied with their initial amount of capital?

Hardly. Before the wage change, the firm was in equilibrium, hiring just enough workers so that $MPP_L P = W$. The firm was also, we may assume, in equilibrium with regard to its employment of capital. This means that it was hiring just enough capital so that $MPP_K \, (K, L) \cdot P = R$, where $MPP_K \, (K, L)$ measures the marginal physical product of capital—the additional output due to an additional unit of capital and R is the price of capital. Following the wage increase, the firm uses less labor. What effect does less labor have on the equilibrium condition for the use of capital? There are now fewer workers per unit of capital (per machine or building): with fewer workers, the marginal product of capital will decrease, since capital has less labor to work with. But if MPP_K falls when L falls, the value of the marginal product of capital $(MMP_K \cdot P)$ will also fall so that it will be below the cost of capital. This, in turn, motivates the firm to reduce employment of capital, which has the effect of reducing MPP_L, thereby leading to a *further decline in the employment of labor*. Eventually the firm will reach a new position with the amount of both resources fulfilling the profit-maximizing or equilibrium condition. The important fact about this new *long-run* position is that fewer workers will be employed than in the short run. *All else being the same*, a firm's response to a change in wages is greater the longer the time allowed for adjustment (Fig. 4–2).

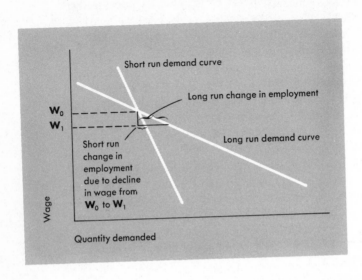

FIG. 4–2 Employment responses to changes in wages in the short run and in the long run.

THE MEANING OF MARGINAL PRODUCTIVITY THEORY

The marginal productivity theory of employment is an abstract model of profit-maximizing employer behavior. It is a *theory* that focuses on some aspects of the employment decision at the expense of others. Because the theory deals only with part of reality you might question its relevance to actual economic behavior. Do profit-maximizing firms change levels of employment according to the theory? In big businesses where managers may have goals beyond simple profit maximization, how do these goals affect employment decisions?

In one sense, even profit-maximizing firms do not behave in accordance with marginal productivity theory—for you will not find businessmen calculating marginal products or pursuing the precise analysis we have developed. However, this does not mean that, in a broader interpretation, the theory is false, for it can still give good predictions of the responsiveness of firms to wage changes. Just as Minnesota Fats need not know the laws of kinetics to put the eight ball in the side pocket, the businessman need not know the ins and outs of marginal productivity to adjust employment toward the profit-maximizing number. The value of the theory lies not in its describing the precise way in which decisions are made but, rather, in its isolating fundamental economic forces and in tracing out their effect.

Indeed, even ignoring the issue of calculating marginal products, firms do not have to behave in the exact manner outlined above for the general results of marginal productivity theory to be valid. Assume, for instance, that the immediate response of a firm to wage increase is to increase its prices rather than to cut employment. This type of behavior—which often involves "marking up" prices by some percentage over long-term cost—is frequently found in manufacturing industries. Does "markup pricing" invalidate the predictions of marginal productivity?

A careful analysis of the eventual effect of wages on employment when firms mark up prices shows general agreement with marginal productivity theory. In a markup model, wage increases lead at first to price increases rather than to employment decreases. What is the effect of these price increases on the sales of the firm and eventually on employment? Price increases, all other things being the same, will reduce sales and, hence, the need for labor. The sequence of responses and the time pattern of adjustment is different in the markup model than in the profit-maximizing marginal productivity model, but the general results are similar: employment depends inversely on wages (Fig. 4–3).

What about employment in firms with goals other than obtaining the highest level of profits possible? Several studies of corporate behavior indicate that in many large firms managers are interested more in making their firm big or in growing rapidly or in arbitrating conflicting interests among stock-holders, employees, and the public than in maximizing profits. Of course, even these firms must earn some profits or at least avoid losses to forestall bank-ruptcy. It is not difficult to see that the desire to use resources efficiently in pursuit of any of these goals guarantees an inverse relation between wages and employment. In the firm desirous of achieving great size, for example, decreases in wages permit an increase in size by hiring additonal workers. Conversely increases in wages raise the cost of achieving the goal by employing many workers and make a reduction of employment and substitution of other inputs for labor sensible. The total number of workers demanded may differ depend-ing on the goals of management but the shape of the demand curve is relatively invariable.

Interpreting "Strange" Results

In 1945 Professor Richard A. Lester of Princeton conducted a question-naire survey of businessmen to find out how important wages are in determining employment.[5] Most businessmen in Lester's survey rated wages as being far less important than "market demand" in their employment decision. Is this

[5]"Shortcomings of Marginal Analysis for Wage–Employment Problems," American Economic Review (March, 1946), pp. 63–82.

	Response to Increased Wages:
Market Model:	Increased wages — — lower employment — — lower output — — higher price
Markup Pricing Model:	Increased wages — — higher price — — lower output — — lower employment
	Response to Decreased Wages:
Market Model:	Decreased wages — — ? — — ? — — ?
Markup Pricing Model:	Decreased wages — — ? — — ? — — ?

FIG. 4–3 A comparison of the market and markup pricing models of employer behavior.

finding inconsistent with the marginal productivity theory of employment or does it agree with the theory?

The survey results can be interpreted in accord with marginal productivity theory in two ways. First, recall that wages are supposed to determine employment when *all else is unchanged*. When the market demand for goods increases, all else is *not* unchanged—indeed, the increase in demand raises the value of the marginal product of labor above its previous level and thereby shifts the demand for labor to the right. A substantial impact of market demand on the derived demand for labor is thus consistent with the theoretic analysis. In fact, it would be strange indeed if businessmen in 1945—when demand changed greatly as a result of the post-World-War-II shift to consumer goods—did not regard "market demand" as the key factor in employment decisions.

An alternative way the survey results can be interpreted into our analysis is in terms of the markup pricing mechanism. If businessmen raise prices when wages increase and this leads to a decline in demand and hence employment, one would expect businessmen to respond as they did to Lester's questionnaire.

MARKET DEMAND FOR LABOR

The preceding discussion has dealt with the demand for labor by an individual firm; however, more than one firm operates in most labor markets. To determine demand in the market, we must examine the aggregate demand by all firms. This requires a slightly more complicated analysis.

The problem in moving from a study of an individual firm's decisions to behavior in the labor market is that some of the variables which are unchanged from the perspective of the firm cannot be regarded as unchanged in the entire market. Specifically, if employers compete in the product market, it would be foolish to ignore the connection between wage changes in the labor market and price and output changes in the product market. A change in wages that induces *all* firms to alter the volume of employment will also change the total output of the industry and ultimately the price of the goods and services produced.

The sequence of events is depicted in Fig. 4–4. At the onset wages in the industry increase from W_0 to W_1, perhaps because of unionization or an increase in minimum wages or a decline in supply due to better job opportunities in other industries. In response to higher wages, each firm reduces employment,

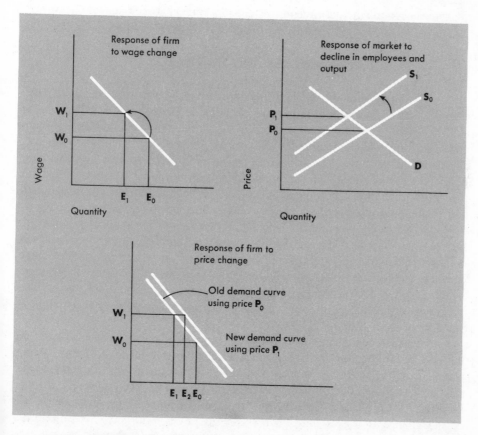

FIG. 4–4 The adjustment of a labor market to a change in wages.

say from E_0 to E_1. With fewer workers, the supply of goods to the product market falls from S_0 to S_1. But a decrease in supply, with consumer demand unchanged, increases the price of output. As a result, firms recompute the marginal value product of workers $(MPP_L\ (L,\ K) \cdot P)$ on the basis of the new market price. Since the price is higher, $MPP_L\ (L,\ K) \cdot P_1$ will be greater than $MPP_L\ (L,\ K) \cdot P_0$, which mitigates the decline in employment resulting from the initial increase in wages.

In other words, when we consider the entire market, an increase in wages disturbing the equilibrium condition $MPP_L\ (L,\ K) \cdot P = W$ is met in two ways: lower L, which increases $MPP_L\ (L,\ K)$ and higher P. The entire adjustment does not fall on employment. *The change in employment in an industry due to a change in wages depends on the change in prices for the product of the firms in the industry and, thus, on the market demand for the product.* There is, you will note, a close parallel between labor market developments in the industry and the "markup pricing" model of the firm presented earlier. In both cases, changes in wages alter employment, output, and prices. As Fig. 4–3 shows, the sequence but not the direction of effects differs between the models.

ECONOMY-WIDE DEMAND FOR LABOR

Analysis of the demand for labor becomes even more complex when the problems of an entire economy are considered. The substantial differences in skill, location, and industrial attachment of workers make it difficult to conceive of a single demand curve for all workers. Even if these factors are ignored, calculation of an aggregate demand curve is tricky because variables that may be viewed as unchanged in analyzing a single firm cannot be so regarded for the entire economy. Consumer demand, in particular, depends on wages and employment throughout the economy and is thus no longer a simple explanatory variable of the demand for labor. Higher wages which reduce employment, for instance, increase the purchasing power of employed persons and their demand for goods and thus increase the demand for labor to produce these goods. At the same time, however, persons who lose their jobs when wages increase will reduce purchases, lowering the derived demand for labor. The net result of the change in wages on the final demand for goods and on employment is not easily estimated.

A further complication relates to the impact of general wage changes on the cost of production and the average level of prices in an economy. When wages in a single firm or market change, it is safe to assume that the living standards of those affected change in the same direction. When all wages change, however, so do all costs and the average level of prices. Part, or perhaps all, of the change in wages may be reflected in prices, with no effect on living standards. In periods of rapid inflation, 1966–69, for example, general increases in money wages are often associated with unchanged or falling living standards, as the change in prices keeps pace or outpaces the change in wages.

A FINAL ISSUE:
FIXED LABOR REQUIREMENTS AND SCALE EFFECTS

One additional difficulty in the analysis of labor demand deserves attention. This is the problem of "fixed labor coefficients," arising out of the joint demand for labor and other inputs. With fixed coefficients, the number of workers is determined by the number of machines in use because each machine requires a definite complement of men or by the number of units of output produced, each of which has a fixed manpower requirement. You recall the earlier example of this situation: the demand for crane operators, which has a one-to-one relation to the number of cranes in service.

When the number of workers needed to operate existing machinery and equipment is set in this way, the demand curve for labor has a peculiar shape.[6] Within a considerable area of wage variation, demand by the firm does not depend on wages. The curve is a vertical line, as in Fig. 4–5A, because a certain number of employees (E) is absolutely essential for production. In the short run at least there is no way to substitute other inputs for labor. When the wage rises above a certain level (W_0), however, the firm begins to lose

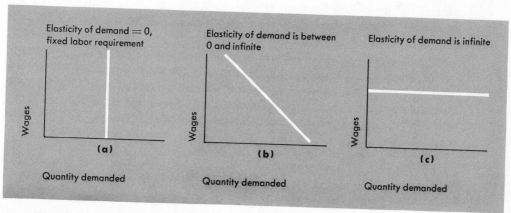

FIG. 4–5 Demand-for-labor curves.

[6]The number of situations to which the fixed requirements model of demand applies may be more limited than at first appears to be the case. This is because even when technology dictates one worker per machine, it is possible to alter the amount of labor used by having multiple shifts, extensive maintenance services, and the like.

money and closes the plant, which cuts the quantity demanded to zero. Until the shutdown point, employment does not respond to wages; thereupon it responds with a vengeance.

The situation of one plant in the short run cannot, however, be generalized to that plant in the long run nor to the entire industry to which it belongs. In the long run it is usually possible for firms to substitute capital for labor through purchases of new equipment and technologies. A construction contractor might, for example, purchase larger or speedier cranes in response to higher wages. As a result the demand for labor will be more elastic as time proceeds.

There are two reasons why industry demand curves will not have zero elasticity even when firms have fixed labor requirements. First, an increase in wages in an entire industry will increase, as noted earlier, the price of output. The higher price will lower the amount of output demanded and reduce production and therefore cut employment. In fact, when there is a fixed link between output and labor "needs," the percentage decline in the number of workers demanded will be exactly equal to the percentage decline in output.[7] The feedback of wages on employment through its impact on prices and output, when the ratio of labor to output or capital is fixed, is called the *scale effect*. It shows that even in the absence of the substitution of other inputs for labor, wage changes influence employment by affecting the scale of production.

The second reason for expecting relatively elastic industry demand for labor schedules is the existence of many plants with different types of equipment in most industries. The wide range of equipment offers substitution possibilities to the market as a whole that do not exist for specific firms. In the market the shutdown for firms will vary widely depending on their machinery. Wage increases will force the least efficient plants, those with the greatest fixed labor requirements, to close down, reducing the demand for labor. With many plants and types of machines, almost any sizeable wage change will have some effect on employment even if each plant has fixed labor requirements. Studies of the machinery used in different plants show great variation in labor requirements, which suggest that market demand curves have relatively smooth downward slopes.

DETERMINANTS OF ELASTICITY

The employment effect of a change in wages is measured, all else remaining fixed, by the shape or elasticity of the demand curve. Knowledge of elasticities is important in understanding the operation of different labor markets. Under what conditions does demand tend to be inelastic? When is it likely to be elastic?

[7]This is easily demonstrated. Let α = the number of workers needed per unit of output; E = number of workers; O = output. Then $E = \alpha O$ and $\Delta E = \alpha \Delta O$. By division we see that $\Delta E / E = \Delta O / O$.

The answer to this question was given by Alfred Marshall who showed that four factors determine the elasticity of demand for labor.[8]

(1) The technological possibility of substituting other inputs for labor in the production process.

The smaller the substitution possibilities for a group of workers, the less elastic is the demand for their services. When substitution is difficult, there are few alternatives to employing the workers beyond going out of business. As a result wage changes will have little impact on employment. In the extreme case of fixed requirements, demand is completely inelastic within a range of alternative wages. In the short run at least certain groups of skilled workers such as airline pilots or doctors face inelastic demand curves because of limited possibilities in substituting machines or other workers for their services. By contrast, the demand for workers for whom good substitutes exist in the production process—say, plasterers who compete with installers of prefabricated plasterboards in construction—tends to be highly elastic. If plasterer wages rise relative to the cost of the dry walls, building contractors will replace the plasterers. In 1965, the Plasterers Union in Philadelphia found that its newly negotiated wage increase had precisely this effect. With employment declining drastically, the union volunteered a wage cut to save jobs.

(2) The elasticity of demand for the goods produced by the laborer.

The less elastic the demand for the output of workers, the less elastic is the derived demand for labor. This is because firms can pass wage changes on to consumers in the form of price increases with little impact on output and, all else being the same, on employment. For example, increases in the wages of workers in rubber-tire factories, which increase tire prices, are likely to reduce the number of tires demanded only slightly, and thus leave the demand for rubber workers relatively fixed. At the opposite end of the spectrum, consider the job impact of changes in the wages of men and women working in New England shoe factories. The demand for New-England-made shoes is extremely elastic because of the possibility of purchasing shoes manufactured in other parts of the United States or from Italy or Switzerland. As a result, wage increases that lead to price increases will reduce the employment of shoe workers substantially, irrespective of possible substitutions of machinery or materials for labor.

(3) The proportion of total costs accounted for by labor costs.

The smaller the ratio of labor costs to total costs, the less elastic, in general, is the demand for labor.[9] When a firm uses capital-intensive methods

---

[8]*Principles of Economics*, 8th ed. (London: Macmillan, 1930), pp. 385–86.

[9]More advanced books show that a smaller ratio of labor to total costs lowers the elasticity of demand for labor only when the possibilities of substituting other commodities for the output of the unionized workers are greater than the possibilities of substituting other factors for unionized workers. In general, it is thought that substitution among commodities is greater than substitution among factor inputs.

of production, changes in wages have only modest effects on costs and thus on prices and the level of production. With labor-intensive technologies, on the other hand, labor cost is the key determinant of prices and output. A 5 percent increase in wages in the oil refining industry, for example, where labor costs are barely 3 percent of total costs, will raise the cost of production by just .15 percent, whereas an equivalent percentage increase in the apparel industry, where the wage bill is 60 percent of total costs, raises cost by 3 percent. All else being the same, the effect of the 5 percent wage gain on prices, output, and ultimately employment will be far greater in apparel than in oil refining plants. Unionized workers in apparel are in a relatively worse position to bargain.

(4) The elasticity of the supply of other inputs.

The smaller the elasticity of the supply of cooperating inputs, the less elastic is the demand for labor. If other inputs cannot be varied at all because their supply is fixed, substitutions that are technologically feasible cannot be made. In the short run when the kind of machines in a plant is given, employers cannot substitute for labor by using more advanced machines with different labor requirements. In the long run, the production of new machinery makes the supply of machines elastic and substitutions possible. The demand for labor is more elastic in the long run rather than in the short run.

The Marshallian determinants of elasticity can be used to estimate the probable consequence of wages on employment. Table 4–1 compares the effect of the determinants on the demand for airline pilots and clothing workers. Because these determinants tend to make demand for pilots more inelastic than that for clothing workers, the power of the Airline Pilots Association to

Table 4–1 DETERMINANTS OF THE ELASTICITY OF DEMAND FOR AIRLINE PILOTS AND CLOTHING WORKERS

	Importance in the demand for	
	Airline Pilots	Clothing Workers
1. Substitutability of other inputs	low	high
2. Elasticity of demand for product of labor	moderate	moderate
3. Proportion of costs spent on labor	very low	very high
4. Elasticity of the supply of other inputs	moderate	moderate
5. Resultant elasticity of demand	low	high
6. Estimated effect of unions on wages	25 + %	<10%

raise wages without seriously disemploying workers will be greater than that of the Amalgamated Clothing Workers. Pilot earnings are likely to be much higher than the earnings of similarly skilled nonunion workers; the wages of clothing workers, on the other hand, are probably only slightly, if at all, above those of comparable nonunion workers. Estimates of the effect of unionization on wages in the last line of the table confirm this prediction: the Pilots Association appears to have raised wages by more than 25 percent, the Clothing Workers, by at most 10 percent.

Shifts in Demand

As time proceeds, changes in consumer demands and in the technology of production alter the demand for labor. Shifts in demand curves rather than movements along curves govern the long-run growth of employment. The principal forces operating the long run are:

1. *The expansion of output.* As an economy develops, output expands rapidly in some industries and slowly in others. Because consumers have limited stomachs and demand for food, the agricultural sector declines relative to manufacturing and services. Because of increased income and changed relative prices, purchases of automobiles, education, and recreation increase markedly. There is a definite pattern to industrial expansion as an economy develops.

The changed composition of output has a major impact on the demand for labor and the kinds of jobs in the economy. About 40 percent of the *relative* growth of employment in engineering from 1900 to 1969, for example, is attributable to the rapid expansion of industries that traditionally employ engineers: professional equipment, aircraft, electrical machinery, and so on. Changes in the kind of workers employed by each industry account for the remaining 60 percent of the increased fraction of the work force in engineering.

2. *Increased productivity.* At the heart of economic growth are increases in labor productivity (output per man-hour of work). Productivity advances unevenly among industries over the long run:

Industry	Change in Output per Man-hour, 1923–1953
Rayon	1217%
Ice cream	341%
Electricity	335%
Pulp and paper mills	184%
Hosiery	172%
Coke	131%
Flour	130%
Bread	117%

The impact of the differential increases in productivity on employment is twofold. All else being the same, industries with large increases in productivity will experience relative declines in employment since fewer workers are needed for production. But all else will not remain the same. An industry with substantial gains in labor productivity will find that labor costs per unit of output and total costs decline rapidly. The decline in cost causes prices to fall and induces consumers to purchase more of the industry's output. Hence, the decline in labor demand associated with the need for fewer workers per unit of output *may be offset* by the increased demand for output. Empirical evidence indicates that over long periods of time the employment-creating effect of the growth of output in progressive industries more than offsets the disemployment effect of rapid productivity gains.

From 1899 to 1953, for example, industries with greater-than-average productivity gains increased their share of total employment from 20 percent to 28 percent. Employment in these industries grew more rapidly than employment elsewhere.[10]

3. *Changes in methods of production.* Finally, demand for labor is affected by long-run changes in the method of production. The introduction of computers into factories and offices, for example, is a major change in technology with serious impacts on the demand for labor. Certain types of workers—programmers, keypunch operators—are needed in great numbers whereas others—bookkeepers and other record keepers—are no longer needed or are required to perform tasks differing from those of the past. The impact of technological change on the relative demand for different kinds of workers is the most difficult long-term force to gauge.

OPERATION OF THE MARKET

Demand does not control wages or employment by itself but simply relates the employment desired by firms to wages. It is the interaction of demand *and* supply that determines the level of wages and employment observed in the labor market.

Figure 4–6 shows how the two schedules jointly regulate wages and employment under differing conditions. In panel *A* the supply of labor is horizontal, indicating that as many workers as desired can be hired at the "going rate." The demand curve tells us how many workers will be hired at that rate. Since most firms employ only a small fraction of the work force, and thus do not seriously affect the "going rate," this is a good description of the situation of individual employers. From the perspective of the firm, the theory of labor demand is a theory of employment.

[10]W. E. G. Salter, *Productivity and Technical Change* (Cambridge University Press, 1966).

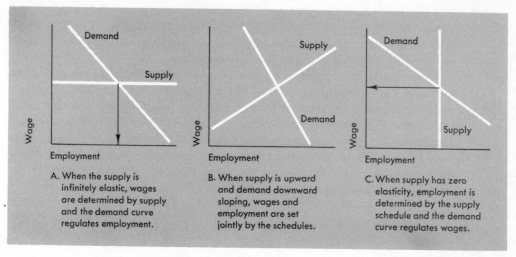

FIG. 4–6   The integration of supply and demand schedules.

A. When the supply is infinitely elastic, wages are determined by supply and the demand curve regulates employment.

B. When supply is upward and demand downward sloping, wages and employment are set jointly by the schedules.

C. When supply has zero elasticity, employment is determined by the supply schedule and the demand curve regulates wages.

An entire labor market—say, the market for coal miners or carpenters—has a different kind of supply schedule. In this case increases in supply will probably require increases in wages. The supply curve is upward sloping and the intersection of supply and demand sets both wages and employment (Fig. 4–6, panel *B*).

Finally, for the economy as a whole, there is a definite limit to the number of workers available. As a rough approximation we might assume that under full employment the supply of labor is completely inelastic. In this case employment depends entirely on the supply curve, whereas the demand curve sets the wage (Fig. 4–6, panel *C*). From the viewpoint of the entire economy, the theory of demand for labor is a theory of wage determination.[11]

SUMMARY

The demand for labor is derived from the demand for goods and services. In any period of time the number of workers demanded by firms is inversely related to wages in the market. The shape of the curve depends on (1) the technological possibilities of substitution; (2) the elasticity of the demand for final goods; (3) the proportion of total costs accounted for by labor costs;

[11]In this context the theory has been used to explain the distribution of national income between labor and other factors. By multiplying the wage by the number of workers, we obtain an estimate of the income paid to labor. Dividing by total GNP yields labor's share of national product.

and (4) the elasticity of the supply of other inputs. As time proceeds, demand curves shift in response to changes in (1) industrial output, (2) increases in productivity, and (3) changes in methods of production. In the market, demand and supply interact to set wages and employment.

The study of demand in this chapter has been relatively abstract. Many important issues regarding wages and employment—the impact of unions, the time required for employees and employers to adjust to new conditions, the effect of government regulations—have been de-emphasized as we have focused on the broad forces determining demand. In Chapter Six, which deals with the specifics of wage determination, some of these complexities are considered more fully. The abstract study of demand provides a clue to the relationships and factors on which a more realistic analysis should focus.

Selected Readings

Bergson, Abram, *Essays in Normative Economics*. Cambridge, Mass.: Harvard University Press, 1966, Chap. 8.

Cartter, Allan M., *Theory of Wages and Employment*. Homewood, Ill.: Richard D. Irwin, 1959.

Hicks, John R., *The Theory of Wages*, 2nd ed. New York: St. Martin's, 1963, Chaps. 1, 2.

Scitovsky, Tibor, *Welfare and Competition*. Homewood, Ill.: Richard D. Irwin, 1971, Part II.

U.S. Department of Labor, *Indexes of Output per Man-Hour, Selected Industries, 1939 and 1947–68*. Bulletin 1652, December, 1969.

Wage Determination and
Economic Well-Being

CHAPTER FIVE

Few labor-market problems are as important to the individual, to the economy, or to society in general as the determination of wages. Wages are the main element of family income. The compensation of employees—wages, salaries, and benefits—constitutes more than 70 percent of total national income. Wages are important in the decisions of individuals to enter the labor market and in the allocation of workers among firms or industries. As a major part of the cost of production, wages help set the level of prices. This chapter examines the economic forces that influences the overall level of wages and the wages paid to different types of workers.

WAGES AND THE PAYMENT FOR LABOR

Remuneration of workers consists of three distinguishable elements of compensation: money wages or salaries paid directly to workers, fringe benefits such as pensions or paid vacations, and non-monetary conditions of work such as location of work, quality of supervision, fellow workers, reputation of the employer, pace of work, and so on.

1. The value of money wages or salaries depends decisively on the availability and price of commodities. When prices change, the remuneration of workers alters even though wages may remain the same.

72

To take account of the changing value of the dollar, a *real wage rate* can be calculated by dividing money wages by an index of consumer prices. The real wage estimates the ability of wages to buy a given selection of goods and services. It distinguishes changes in wages that increase purchasing power from those that merely keep pace with inflation and is thus a better indicator of economic well-being over a period of years than are money wages.

An illustrative computation makes clearer the distinction between real and money wages:

> In 1959 the average hourly earnings of manufacturing workers was $2.19. In 1969, earnings rose to $3.03 per hour, a gain in money wages of 84¢, or 38 percent of the initial wage. Consumer prices also rose from 1959 to 1969: goods and services that cost $1 in 1959 were estimated by the Bureau of Labor Statistics to cost $1.26 in 1969. Roughly speaking a 1969 dollar was worth just .79 (=1.00/1.26) 1959 dollars. In terms of ability to purchase commodities at 1959 prices, average hourly earnings in 1969 were worth $2.40 (=3.03/1.26). The change in *real* wages in this ten-year period was 10 percent of the base rate; the remaining gain in money wages was needed to keep pace with inflation.

2. Fringe benefits or supplementary payments are an increasingly important component of compensation in the United States. Table 5–1 illustrates the importance of fringes relative to wages and salaries in more than 1000 large United States companies, according to a survey by the Chamber of Commerce of the United States. Nearly a quarter of total compensation consists of fringes, with pension plans, vacation and holiday pay, and insurance protection the main privately determined fringes and Social Security, workmen's compensation, and unemployment compensation the main legally required expenses.

3. Conditions of work include such non-monetary features of a job as its location, parking facilities, reputation of the firm in the locality, congeniality of the work force, physical facilities and air conditioning, quality of supervision, recreational programs, and other features of the work environment. These work conditions are often decisive to workers in their choices among jobs and their attachment and productivity on the job. To call such conditions "nonmonetary" is in part a misnomer since many cost the enterprise a good deal of money and affect the total income, or the take-home pay, of workers. When economists compare the relative compensation of jobs, they presume that these working conditions are relatively equal. In real life such equality seldom, if ever, exists.

The General Level of Wages: Long-Term Trends

You are likely to earn more than your parents did at your age. They probably earned more than their parents. Over the long run money wages and

Table 5–1 THE COMPENSATION PACKAGE IN 1969: FRINGE BENE-
FITS IN LARGE COMPANIES AS A PERCENTAGE OF PAYROLL EX-
PENSES

Total fringe payments as percent of payroll	27.9%
1. Legally required payments (employer's share only)	6.4
a. Old age, survivors, and disability insurance	4.6
b. Unemployment compensation	0.8
c. Workmen's compensation	0.9
d. Railroad retirement tax; railroad, unemployment insurance, state sickness benefits insurance etc.	0.1
2. Pension and other agreed-upon payment (employer's share only)	8.3
a. Pension-plan premiums and pension payments not covered by insurance type plan (net)	4.2
b. Life insurance premiums; death benefits; sickness, accident, and medical care insurance premiums; hospitalization insurance; etc. (net)	3.5
c. Others, including employee meals furnished by company, discounts on company goods, etc.	0.6
3. Paid rest periods, lunch periods, washup time, travel time, clothes change time, get-ready time, etc.	2.9
4. Payments for time not worked	8.3
a. Paid vacation and bonuses in lieu of vacation	4.4
b. Payments for holidays not worked	2.7
c. Others, including paid sick leave, etc.	1.2
5. Other items:	2.0
a. Paid vacation and bonuses in lieu of vacation	4.4
b. Christmas or other special bonuses	0.5
c. Others, including contributions to employee thrift plans, etc.	0.3

Source: "Employee Benefits, 1969" research study by economic analysis and study group. Chamber of Commerce of the United States, Table 4.

real wages have increased greatly in the United States. Since 1900 total compensation per hour in manufacturing has increased almost 20 times.[1] This represents a cumulative rate of increase of 4.5 percent a year. In the same period consumer prices increased almost threefold; this represents a cumulative rate of increase of 2 percent a year. Thus, real wage rates have increased at a cumulative rate of about 2.5 percent a year during this century.

The upward trend in money wages and in real wages proceeded unevenly over time. In some decades, money rates hardly changed at all so that increases or decreases in real income were due to changes in prices; at other times, inflation outpaced wage gains. In the 1870's and again in the early years of the Great Depression, money wages and prices declined whereas real wages remained roughly the same. Since the Depression the likelihood of substantial wage cuts has been lessened by the expansionary policies of the government

74

[1]Total compensation per hour of work in manufacturing was $.15 per hour in 1900; $.553 per hour in 1920; $.67 per hour in 1940; $1.41 per hour in 1948; and $3.54 per hour in 1971.

and the opposition of trade unions. The diverse wage–price experience of the United States since Civil War days is illustrated below:

| Period | Annual Percentage Change | | |
	Money Earnings	Prices	Real
1860–1870	+35%	+57%	−18%
1870–1880	−20%	−23%	+5%
1880–1890	+22%	−6%	+31%
1890–1900	−1%	−13%	+10%
1900–1910	31%	+12%	17%
1910–1920	125%	+111%	11%
1920–1930	5%	−17%	26%
1930–1940	−7%	−17%	11%
1940–1950	134%	+72%	36%
1950–1960	62%	+23%	31%
1960–1970	57%	31%	21%

Sources: 1860–1960—S. Legergott, *Manpower in Economic Growth* (New York: McGraw-Hill, 1964), *Monthly Labor Review, Survey of Current Business.*

What explains the upward trend in real wages in the United States?

The simplest response, though not a very profound one, is that the demand for labor has increased greatly in relation to the supply of workers (Fig. 5–1). Underlying the relative increase in demand are several economic develop-

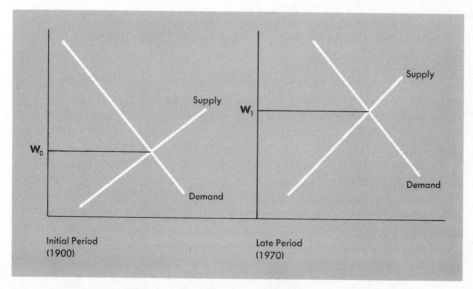

FIG. 5–1 The effect of shifts in the demand and supply of labor on wages.

ments whose unfolding offers a more meaningful explanation of the trend in wages. Of great significance is the increased quality and quantity of resources available to workers in the production process and the growth of consumer demand for the output of the economy (see Table 5–2).

Increased capital per worker. From 1900 to 1968 the value of physical capital in manufacturing increased from $2164 to $8700 per worker. Technological advances such as the computer improved the quality of capital. With more and better capital the productivity of labor increases, and in a growth economy the demand for labor shifts upward to the right.

Additional nonhuman energy. In 1900 when horses were a major source of nonhuman energy, a manufacturing worker received about 8 horsepower hours of nonhuman work per hour of employment. In 1970, with electrical, nuclear, and other energy sources, 75 horsepower hours of nonhuman energy were available to workers in manufacturing—9½ times that available at the turn of the century.

Higher-quality labor. The long-term increase in the education and skill of workers also enhanced productivity and wages. From 1900 to 1970 the average number of years of schooling in the United States more than doubled. It has been estimated that 25 to 40 percent of the long-term increase in product per worker is associated with increased education.

Scientific and technical advance. The application of science and technology to economic problems distinguishes the United States economy in the twentieth century from past societies. At the turn of the century there were perhaps 60,000 scientists and engineers; in 1970 more than 1,600,000. Many

Table 5–2 FACTORS INCREASING THE PRODUCTIVITY AND REAL WAGES OF WORKERS

	1900	1968
Physical capital per worker in manufacturing industries (in dollars per worker)	2164	8700
Horsepower energy per worker (in horsepower hours)	21,800	150,000
Years of schooling per worker*	5.2	12.3
Scientists and engineers per thousand workers	0.5	22
Fraction of the work force in agriculture	37.5%	4.3%

*Assuming 160 days of school per year.

Source: U.S. Bureau of the Census, *Historical Statistics of the United States* (Washington, U.S.G.P.O., 1960). U.S. Bureau of the Census, *Statistical Abstract 1969* (Washington, U.S.G.P.O.)

of the new and improved produts of industry are ultimately based on scientific or engineering advances: rayon, commercial airplanes, television, and so on.

Expansion of High-Productivity Industries. The productivity of labor is high in some sectors of the economy—such as capital-intensive manufacturing industries—and relatively low in agriculture. Part of the long-term increase in productivity and real wages is due to the shift of workers from low- to high-productivity industries. In 1900, 38 percent of the work force was employed in agriculture, where earnings are just 30 percent of those in manufacturing. By 1970, only 4 percent of the work force remained in agriculture. Approximately one-sixth of the increased real wage and product per worker is associated with the movement of labor to industries with greater productivity.

The Growth of Aggregate Demand. Sustaining all these trends has been the increased demand for goods and services that is part and parcel of a growing economy. Without increased spending by consumers, various levels of government, and business firms, the economy would stagnate. Potential gains in productivity would be wasted in unwanted goods or displaced workers.

The Role of Supply

Conceivably, as Malthus feared, the supply af labor could grow so rapidly that wages would be forced to low levels despite greater demand from workers. A necessary condition for increasing real income is that the population and labor supply expand at less than Malthusian rates. In the United States and Western Europe, though not in some less-developed countries, such has been the case. As a result of declines in birth rates, the population in developed lands is growing less rapidly than in Asia, Latin America, and Africa. Even so, continuous increases in the supply of persons in the United States and Europe have created serious population-related problems in traffic, pollution, and so on and may produce greater difficulties in the future.

Wages, Prices, and Productivity in the Short Run

Consider the following problem: the rate of unemployment in the economy is 5.2 percent, with a concentration of jobless among nonwhites (9.8 percent), laborers (10.6 percent), and teenagers (16.2 percent). The level of prices has been virtually constant for many years. To reduce unemployment, the government undertakes a series of measures which increase aggregate demand: taxes are cut, additional dollars are spent for construction of houses, interest rates are lowered, and the money supply increased. The economy responds favorably to this expansionary policy; within a few years, unemployment drops to 3.6 percent. But prices begin to rise at 5 percent per year. In the next few years, the price rise accelerates to 6 percent per year and unemployment begins increasing. What economic policy is appropriate for this economy?

This situation—a rough description of the state of the United States

77

economy at the onset of 1971—illustrates the conflict between full employment and price stability that has concerned the United States throughout much of the decade of the sixties. Policies designed to reduce unemployment by increasing aggregate demand had the undesirable effect of inducing price increases; policies restraining total spending for purposes of price stability also restrained the demand for labor and were accompanied by unemployment. For whatever basic cause or causes, price stability and full employment seemed incompatible in the sixties.

Wages are at the center of the unemployment–inflation dilemma. Increases in the demand for labor that reduce unemployment are likely to raise money wages. If these wage gains exceed the normal increase in labor productivity, the cost of labor per unit of output, and ultimately prices, will rise.[2] An unpleasant choice between inflation and unemployment must be made when the increase in prices commences before full employment is attained.

How important is the unemployment–inflation dilemma? What levels of unemployment are associated with inflationary or noninflationary wage increases? What policies might reduce unemployment while preserving wage-price stability?

Unemployment–Wage Change Curves

The effect of unemployment on money wages has been studied intensively by economists. The studies show that when unemployment is low or falling, money wages rise more rapidly than when unemployment is high or rising (Fig. 5–2). With low rates of unemployment the wage demands of unions and the willingness of members to strike are high. Striking workers are often able to obtain temporary jobs in a tight labor market. Employers are willing to grant large wage increases to avoid a stop in production that will lose sales. In nonunion markets employers who expand output must raise wages to attract workers from other firms. The entire situation is reversed when unemployment rates are high, with high unemployment being associated with relatively slow wage increases. The tradeoff between unemployment and inflation thus appears to be unfavorable: less unemployment means rising wages and prices; less inflation means more unemployment.

Figure 5–2 depicts the unemployment–wage change relation for the United States in the period 1947–1971. Each point along the *Phillips curve* (named after its originator) represents the rate of unemployment and change in money wages in a particular year. The configuration of points shows that

[2]To see how wages and productivity affect cost, note that by definition unit labor costs (ULC) equals the wage (W) multiplied by the number of workers used per unit of output (L/O): $ULC = W \cdot L/O = W/(O/L)$.

Where L = number of workers; O = output; and O/L = labor productivity. From the equation it is clear that equal percentage increases in W and (O/L) do not alter unit labor costs while wage gains in excess of productivity gains increase ULC.

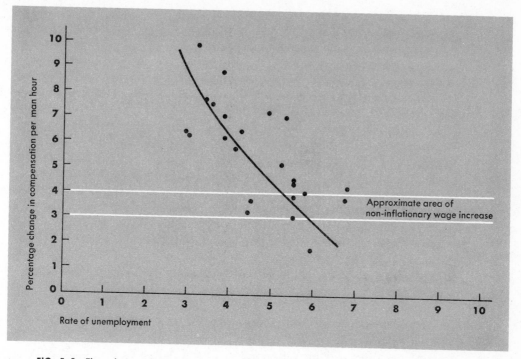

FIG. 5–2 The relation of unemployment to changes in money wages in the United States, 1947–1971.

unemployment and money wages are *loosely* related. Although on the average wages rise more rapidly when unemployment is low, the Phillips curve does not tell us the precise rate of change at each level. An unemployment rate of 5.5 percent of the total labor force in 1954 was, for example, associated with a 3 percent increase in money wages whereas similar unemployment in 1959, 1960, and 1962 resulted in wage changes of 4.6, 3.9, and 4.4 percent, respectively.

Obviously unemployment is not the only variable influencing money wages. Other factors—notably the rate of *profits* in industry and the level of *consumer prices*—also help determine the wage level.

Profits are likely to affect wages in two ways. In unionized industries, high profits are a good indicator of management's ability to increase wages and of the cost to the firm of a strike. Unions pay close attention to profits in negotiations, and are likely to raise their wage demands when profits are high. In both union and nonunion industries, moreover, high profits will often induce

79

established firms to expand output and new firms to enter, shifting the demand for labor upward to the right.

As a result, wages tend to increase more rapidly when profits are high than when they are low. For example, in the five years with the highest rates of profits in the postwar period, hourly compensation rose on the average by 7.8 percent per year compared to 3.9 percent in the five years with the lowest rates of profit.

Consumer prices have a dual relation to money wages. On the one hand, wages help set the level of prices by affecting labor costs. On the other, individual workers and unions demand higher wages when inflation eats away purchasing power. Some economists, in fact, argue that because workers are concerned solely with real wages, they will demand increases in wages that just counterbalance the loss of real income that they *expect* from inflation. If this is the case and if workers succeed in escalating wages, the Phillips curve shifts upward in inflationary times, worsening the unemployment inflation dilemma (Fig. 5–3).

Assume, for example, that initially there is no inflation and that a 4 percent rate of unemployment is associated with a 5½ percent rate of increase in wages in a given year. This wage increase far exceeds the normal gain in labor productivity of 3½ percent per year and thus increases prices by about 2 percent. The ensuing reduction in purchasing power presumably leads workers to expect additional inflationary losses in the future. To offset future inflation and to recoup the unexpected loss in earning power due to the 2 percent price increase, workers will demand more-rapid increases in wages. As a result the rate of change in wages will accelerate from 5½ percent until

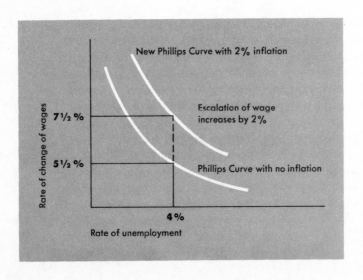

FIG. 5–3 Possible wage-price interactions shifting the Phillips curve upward in inflationary times.

it eventually reaches 7½ percent [= 5½% + 2%]. With a 2 percent inflation and a 7½ percent increase in wages workers will obtain the 5½ percent gain they originally anticipated. But the increase in the rate of change of wages will cause additional inflation, which leads to additional wage demands, and so on. The Phillips curve relating wage increases to unemployment rises, as in Figure 5–3, and the wage–price spiral takes over.

If this argument is valid, there is no stable tradeoff between inflation and unemployment. In the short run there exists a tradeoff, which is reflected in a Phillips curve. But in the long run the curve rises horizontally so that policies that reduce unemployment at the cost of inflation produce an accelerating rate of inflation.

Not all economists accept the argument that inflation increases money wages by the same rate as the increase in prices. Since workers bargain individually or in unions for money wages, some claim that workers are primarily concerned with the money wage rate. Others note that adjusting to inflation involves real costs which make labor supply responses to moderate changes in prices unlikely. It may not pay, for example, to demand higher wages or quit your job in search of a better paying position when prices rise by one percent. Finally, the real wages that workers expect may change as economic circumstances change. In a period of severe inflation the expected gain in real wages may drop (say, from the 5 percent expected with 4 percent unemployment and no inflation to 4 percent), as workers find real wage gains below previous expectations.

Empirical studies of the impact of inflation on wage increases tend to support the argument that money wages do not completely adjust to inflation. Most calculations show that a one percent increase in prices or in the prices people can be reasonably expected to foresee produces an increase in money wages of less than one-half percent. If this is true, the Phillips curve does not shift up by one percent per one percent increase in prices as in Fig. 5–3, but by about one-half percent. As a result the rate of inflation decelerates rather than accelerates over time: a two percent inflation raises wage demands by one percent over what they would otherwise be, which increases the rate of change of prices by at most an additional one percent, causing a one-half percent increase in wage demands and so on.[3] Under these circumstances, there is a stable long-run tradeoff between prices and wages.

Because of the interdependence between wages and prices—the fact that each significantly affects the other—and because of the complexities of price and wage determination in an industrial economy, however, it is difficult to

[3]From your high-school algebra you will note that the impact of prices on wages in this case produces a geometric series, which converges to a single number. The series 2%, 1%, ½% converges to 4%, which is the eventual increase in inflation resulting from the policies that reduced unemployment by one percentage point.

know how much weight to place on the empirical studies. Certainly no one would deny that consumer prices are an important determinant of money wages. As the following figures show, there is a strong association between rates of change in these variables: in the years of substantial inflation money wages rise rapidly; in years of slight price increases, wages advance slowly:

Years of Greatest Postwar Inflation	Change in Consumer Prices Index	Change in Compensation Per Man-Hour
1947–1948	+7.7%	8.8
1950–1951	8.0	9.9
1968–1969	6.4	7.8
1969–1970	5.6	7.2
Years of Smallest Postwar Inflation		
1948–1949	−1.0	1.7
1953–1954	0.4	3.0
1954–1955	−0.3	3.2
1958–1959	0.8	4.6

The best way in which to interpret these relations and the precise link of inflation to the Phillips curve remain matters of controversy. In view of their importance to economic policy, it is safe to say that additional theoretical and empirical work will be undertaken on these issues in the future.

WAGE STRUCTURES AND LABOR MOBILITY

Wages and salaries differ widely among the thousands of jobs in an industrial economy. Some occupations and industries offer high pay whereas earnings in others are relatively low. Many doctors and some airline pilots, for example, earned more than $30,000 in 1970 while most laborers and hospital attendants made less than $5,000. In the oil industry, average hourly earnings were on the order of $4; in firms making women's undergarments, production workers received just $2.25 per hour.

Differences in wages such as those between M.D.'s and hospital attendants or oil workers and ladies' garment workers do not arise by chance. In a free labor market, wage differentials guide the allocation of workers among occupations, industries, and localities. The pattern of wages reflects the basic supply and demand relations in the economy and is an important indicator of labor scarcities or surpluses. The differential between high- and low-paid workers helps determine the distribution of income.

We explore next some of the principal dimensions of wage differentials in the United States: occupational and industrial wage structures, differentials due to union wage pressures; and white–nonwhite income differentials.

Occupational Differentials

Skilled workers tend to be paid more than less-skilled workers, particularly in the same enterprise and industry. Craftsmen are higher paid than laborers; engineers receive more than technicians; and so on. It is not difficult to see why skilled workers receive a premium, for they have invested time, effort, and money (often in the form of income foregone) to learn to perform some useful task. Without a return on this investment, relatively few would undertake the requisite education or training.[4] The high earnings of the doctor are, in part, payment for the years of education when he receives little or no pay and for his direct outlays to medical schools.

Since the turn of the century the percentage wage differential between high- and low-skill workers has declined markedly[5] particularly in periods of wartime. Roughly, skilled men in factories received twice the pay of unskilled men in 1900 compared to about a 30 percent differential today.

The principal cause of the secular decline in the premium for skill appears to be the increased supply of skilled as compared with unskilled persons. All else being the same, a relative increase in the number of skilled workers must reduce the skill premium (Fig. 5–4). In the United States the shift in supply is due to such factors as

—the tremendous expansion of education at the high-school and college levels
—restrictive immigration laws that reduced the supply of unskilled immigrants
—the declining importance of rural areas as "producers" of unskilled workers
—intensive on-the-job-training programs in all kinds of enterprises

Underlying the expansion of education and investment in on-the-job training is the high return on these forms of human capital.

The long-term trend toward lower skill differentials seems to have come to a halt in the 1950's and 1960's and in some instances to have been reversed. From 1957 to 1967, workers in highly-skilled professions—doctorate scientists and engineers, university professors, physicians and surgeons, and other specialists—enjoyed greater percentage increases in wages than other workers. In some industries or localities, the differential of craftsmen and laborers and janitors widened; in others, it narrowed but slightly. Economists are not sure of the reason for the break in the movement toward narrower differentials.

---

[4]More precisely, recall from the discussion in Chapter Three (pp. 42–44) that the supply decision of marginal workers, not of all persons, is affected by wages. Thus the relevant differential between skilled and unskilled workers is the differential required by marginal suppliers. Of course, as the number of persons demanded increases and more are attracted into an occupation, the people "on the margin" change.

[5]See Mark W. Leiserson, "Wage Decisions and Wage Structure in the United States," in E. M. Hugh-Jones, ed., Wage-Structure in Theory and Practice (Amsterdam: North-Holland Publishing Company, 1966), pp. 1–70.

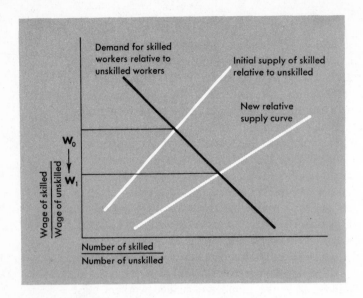

FIG. 5-4 The effect of a relative increase in the supply of skilled to unskilled workers on occupational wage differentials.

In part, widening of differentials in some sectors may be a delayed response to the very narrow differentials created by government wage regulation during World War II. In other sectors skill differentials—say, those between tool and diemakers and laborers in machinery manufacturing—may have approached the minimum necessary to induce marginal workers into the skilled job. Large increases in the salaries of scientists and engineers, university professors, and related professionals in the sixties can be attributed to the shift in demand for these personnel arising from the space program and the growth of the higher-educational system. The relative cutback in federal research- and development spending in the late 1960's–early 1970's drastically shifted the market against these specialists and began narrowing their differential relative to the less-skilled.

Industrial Differentials

Across the world, workers in petroleum- or coal-refining plants earn more than workers in the apparel industry:

	Petroleum Refining	Apparel	Units of Pay (1967)
United States	$ 3.58	$ 2.03	Dollars per hour
Japan	676.69	266.95	Yen per month
India	262.70	162.10	Rupees per month
Hungary	18.56	15.18	Forints per month
Poland	24.11	16.13	Zlotys per month
Italy	6.41	3.44	Lire per hour
Columbia	8.34	3.16	Pesos per hour

Why is it that regardless of economic system or method of wage payment petroleum and coal refineries outpay clothing plants? What factors explain interindustrial wage differentials?

The technology of production, which is relatively invariant across countries in industries such as petroleum refining or clothing, is the key determinant of the industrial wage structure. In every country, refining plants employ relatively more-skilled workers than clothing manufacturers. As a result pay is uniformly higher in petroleum irrespective of institutional or ideological differences. Table 5–3 shows the differences in occupational structures for these industries in the United States.

Technological revolutions that completely alter the kind of work performed in an industry are relatively infrequent. Industries which are skill-intensive at one period of time tend to be skill-intensive in later years. For this reason the industrial wage structure is quite stable over time. In the 1910's the highest-paying manufacturing industries were (in order to their rate of pay): primary metals, transportation equipment, machinery, petroleum and coal refining, and printing and publishing. The same five are found at the top of the industrial wage structure in 1970; though in slightly different order. At the bottom of the structure the story is the same: industries such as lumber products, tobacco, and textiles were low-paying in 1910 and 1970.

While general stability is the rule for the industrial wage structure, specific industries change their position in response to differing economic situations. Industries in which the demand for labor declines drastically tend to fall in the wage structure. New and expanding industries often offer relatively high wages to attract workers. When firms that manufacture airplane engines grew

Table 5–3   THE SKILL COMPOSITION OF THE WORK FORCE IN THE PETROLEUM AND CLOTHING INDUSTRIES

Occupation	Percentage Distribution of the Work Force	
	Petroleum Refining	Apparel
Highly Skilled	45.9	9.6
Professional	16.2	1.1
Managerial	6.0	3.7
Craftsmen	23.7	4.8
Semiskilled	46.6	88.6
Clerical	18.1	7.1
Sales workers	2.2	2.3
Operatives	26.3	79.2
Unskilled	7.7	1.7
Laborers and service workers	7.7	1.7

Source: U.S. Census of Population, 1960.

rapidly from 1950 to 1968, for example, the average earnings of their employees increased by 4.7 percent per year compared to a gain of 4.3 percent for workers in other manufacturing enterprises. By contrast, when aircraft employment and output declined greatly in the leather shoe industry, wages fell relative to those in other industries. In 1950 the average shoe worker earned 23% less than other manufacturing workers; in 1968 he earned 28% less.

According to the economic theory of markets, when the labor market is in equilibrium, similarly skilled workers receive equivalent compensation from alternative employers. Industries with unpleasant working conditions such as steel or coal will pay large money wages to offset the nonmonetary disadvantage. Industries with pleasant conditions will be able to obtain workers at lower rates. If the demand for labor rises sharply in an industry and wages increase beyond the equilibrium level, additional workers will seek jobs in that industry, shifting the supply of labor upward to the right. The shift in supply in time reduces wages toward their equilibrium level (Fig. 5–5). Labor

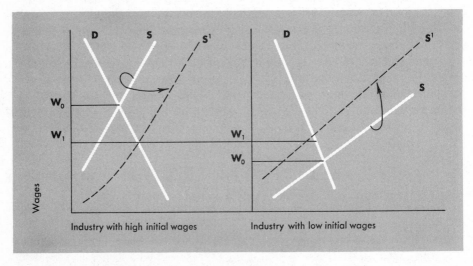

FIG. 5–5 The elimination of industrial wage differentials by labor mobility.

mobility thus acts as a check on the wage structure, keeping rates in different sectors of the economy in line with economic reality. Most studies of labor mobility find a modest positive association between rates of increase in wages and employment, indicating that small adjustments in the wage structure facilitate the redistribution of labor among industries in accord with the market theory.

86

The Union Wage Effect

Every year thousands of union officials representing millions of workers negotiate wages and working conditions with the management of large and small firms. Newspapers report "union wins 8 percent wage gain" or "union settled for 3 percent." The vast majority of Americans believe that the gains workers have made in this country are chiefly due to labor unions. A public opinion poll in 1960 asked the general public the question: "Do you agree that the gains that workers have made in this country are chiefly due to unions?" The answers were as follows:

Gains due to unions   66%
Gains not due to unions 17%
Don't know   17%

There is a natural tendency for labor leaders, management, and the public to attribute wage increases to the influence of trade unions and collective bargaining. It is far easier to credit or blame a union or union leader for wage changes than the impersonal forces of supply and demand. A dramatic negotiation or strike is more newsworthy than a gradual change in technology or consumer spending patterns that shifts the demand for labor. "But appearances may deceive. In the fable of Cantillon the cock flapped its wings and crowed each morning as the sun emerged over the horizon, and eventually persuaded himself that he alone was responsible for the sunrise. There is a good deal in the ritual, chest-thumping, and crowing in collective bargaining negotiations that is reminiscent of Cantillon's fable."

It is difficult to obtain a scientific estimate of the actual effect of the union movement on wages. Organization of workers and the development of collective bargaining change many aspects of the work relation in addition to the level of wages. The rules of work, methods of supervision, promotion, and wage payments are altered; productivity is affected. By modifying the entire market environment unions alter wages throughout the economy as well as the wages of members.

Despite these complexities, several attempts have been made to estimate the wage effect of particular unions and of unionization in general. The methodology of the studies is direct: compare wages or changes in wages of workers likely to be greatly affected by unions with those of workers only slightly affected. One study, for example, contrasts the wages of transit workers in predominantly unionized cities with those in unorganized cities. Differences in wages are attributed to the presence of collective bargaining. Obviously these calculations are crude and provide at best rough estimates of the order of magnitude of the union wage effect. In the social sciences, you cannot eliminate a critical institution like collective bargaining from the economy to observe its impact. Many factors influence wages for which it is difficult to account: supplies and demands continually change in a dynamic economy; unorganized employers may raise wages or offer very high wages and attractive employment conditions in part to forestall unionization (Eastman Kodak and IBM, for example).

Approximate and tentative though they are, the union–nonunion wage comparisons have at least one important implication for the operation of the labor market. They suggest that the influence of collective bargaining on the level of wages is not as great as is often claimed. In the most comprehensive review of the statistical evidence, Professor H. G. Lewis of the University of Chicago concluded that the strongest unions (construction crafts, United Mine Workers, among others) raise the wages of members by 15 to 25 percent above the wages of similarly skilled nonunion workers.[6] Weaker unions, which have not completely organized their jurisdiction or which are threatened by the actual or potential competition of nonunion employers or products, have wage effects on the order of 0 to 5 percent. The elasticity of demand for these workers is too great to permit large union wage premium.

The greatest differential between the average union wage and the average nonunion wage—25 percent—occurred in the Great Depression when unions blocked wage cuts. Contrary to popular opinion, the union wage differential appears to decline dramatically in periods of rapid inflation; Lewis estimated the average effect to be no more than 5 percent in the period 1945 to 1949. During the inflation of the last half of the 1960's, for example, the largely unorganized industries of agriculture, services, and retail trade showed much greater wage increases than the highly organized manufacturing sector. Within manufacturing the least organized industries had the largest percentage gains. Although the performance of the unionized sector might have indirectly influenced unorganized industries, it is difficult to attribute the major inflationary force to the ability of unions to enforce "excessive" wage increases. The tightening of labor markets had an important influence on wage changes in this period.

Labor-Market Discrimination

Discrimination in the labor market against certain persons such as nonwhites or women operates in many ways. Employers may prefer whites to nonwhites of equal ability when white and nonwhite wages are equal. To obtain employment the group being discriminated against is obligated to accept lower wages or the least attractive jobs. Discrimination also operates through the purchasing decisions of consumers, who may refuse to buy in stores that employ members of minority groups. Union restrictions in jobs where the union controls hiring policies or apprenticeship and training programs is another way in which discrimination may limit opportunities. Finally, the educational system has for

[6]*Unionism and Relative Wages in the United States* (Chicago: University of Chicago Press, 1963).

many years provided especially poor opportunities for nonwhites. Low-quality education makes the employment of minorities in better jobs extremely difficult. The employer with no desire to discriminate will often find it economically rational to hire the better educated (white) as opposed to the less educated (nonwhite).

In addition to discrimination, other factors also operate against minority workers. In many cases, nonwhites lack information about job opportunities because much of the knowledge about jobs is conveyed by informal and personal contacts with present employees, who may be white. The absence of adequate transportation and the distance between job and residence also serves as a barrier to employment prospects.

The effect of discrimination and related factors on the economic status of nonwhite Americans is shown in Table 5–4. The picture for nonwhite males is an arresting one. They earn barely 70 percent of the earnings of white males. They are concentrated in the lowest-paying and least-pleasant jobs in the society, and in the same broad occupational categories earn at most 80 percent of whites. Even with the same years of education, nonwhite males still earn noticeably less than white males. Indeed, perhaps the most striking fact about income differentials by race is the evidence that nonwhite college graduates have traditionally earned less than white high-school graduates!

Part of the differential between black and white men is due to the different

Table 5–4 OCCUPATIONAL DISTRIBUTION AND EARNINGS, BY RACE, 1968

| | Percentage Distribution of Employment | | | | Median Earnings of Blacks Relative to Whites (full-time, year-round workers) | |
| | Black* | | White | | | |
	Male	Female	Male	Female	Male	Female
All	100	100	100	100	0.68	0.76
Professional and technical	7	10	14	15	0.74	0.97
Managerial	4	2	15	5	0.56	—
Clerical	7	18	7	36	0.87	0.93
Sales	2	2	6	8	—	—
Craftsmen and foremen	18	1	21	1	0.75	—
Operatives	28	17	19	15	0.76	0.84
Service workers, except household	14	25	6	14	0.72	0.96
Private household workers	—	20	—	4	—	0.98
Nonfarm laborers	18	1	6	—	0.80	—
Farmers and farm workers	7	2	6	2	0.61	—

*In this case, the data are for all nonwhites. Since blacks constitute 92 percent of the nonwhite population, it is reasonable to use the nonwhite figures to measure black status. Source: U.S. Department of Commerce, Current Population Reports: Series 1–60 No. 66; Handbook of Labor Statistics.

MEDIAN INCOME OF MEN 25 YEARS AND OVER, 1968

Years of Schooling	White Males	Black Males
Elementary school	$ 5,184	$4,261
High School	7,875	5,721
College	12,667	7,351

Source: U.S. Department of Commerce, Consumer Income. College figures estimated from "4 or more years" of college using national averages.

occupational compositions of the two work forces. Part is associated with income differences within occupations. One way of estimating the relative importance of these two factors is to take a weighted average of nonwhite incomes by occupation, where the weights are the fraction of whites working in the occupation.[7] This average shows what nonwhites would earn if they were distributed among occupations in the same proportion as whites but were paid the current nonwhite rate. Such a calculation for 1968 reveals that the bulk of the nonwhite–white male differential in that year was attributable to intraoccupational income differences. Nonwhite male incomes would have been only 8 percent higher than they actually were if nonwhites were employed in the same proportion as whites among occupations. A major reason for this is the position of black managers in the income hierarchy. As Table 5–4 shows, the absolute and relative pay of black managers has been extraordinarily low, primarily because of their historic exclusion from major corporations.

The situation of black women is quite different, for within broadly defined occupational (or educational) classes, they do roughly as well as their white counterparts. Indeed, because black women are more likely to hold full-time jobs, the income of all black women (not, as in the table, those with full-time positions) exceeds that of whites in several areas. In 1968, for example, black female college graduates reported $6,275 in median income compared to $5,301 for white graduates. On the basis of these facts, it is apparent that black women could attain overall income equality with whites by increased educational or occupational skills.

Changes Over Time

The labor market position of nonwhite Americans improved in the 1960–70 decade. At the onset of the sixties nonwhite family incomes were about 52 percent of white families' compared to 61 percent in the late sixties. Unemployment of nonwhite adult males was about 10 percent in 1960 compared to 3.9 percent in 1969. An increasing number of nonwhites were able to obtain the educational and occupational skills that lead to economic advance-

[7]Let α_1 = number of whites in occupation i divided by the total number of whites and let W_i = nonwhite incomes in occupation i. Then $w = \Sigma \alpha_1 w_i$ is an estimate of the income nonwhites would receive if they had the same occupational distribution as whites but were paid at nonwhite rates of pay.

ment. For example, the number holding teaching positions exclusive of college increased from 6.5 percent to 9.4 percent of the teaching work force in the period 1957 to 1967; the number employed as managers rose from 2.9 percent to 4.4 percent of the managerial work force; the number of nonwhite carpenters increased from 3.9 percent to 6.2 percent of that occupation, and so on.[8]

The improvement in economic status was greatest for women and for young men just starting their careers. As Fig. 5–6 shows, the ratio of black to white wages and salaries among women has risen steadily since the end of World War II, with the resultant attainment of rough equality within skill classes today.[9] For young men, especially those with higher education, the labor market began changing markedly in the late 1960's. For the first time, major corporations began to recruit black men for high-paying professional and managerial jobs. In 1965 virtually no company travelled to the Southern black colleges to interview job candidates; in 1970 most major companies interviewed and hired black graduates from these and other colleges.[10] Overall, the ratio of nonwhite to white incomes for men aged 20 to 24 jumped from 0.67 in 1959 to 0.79 in 1970.

By contrast, the increase in the relative income of *all* nonwhite men in the sixties was slight and may have been the result largely of cyclic conditions. Historically, as Fig. 5–6 shows, the relative income of black men has fluctuated considerably, with some tendency to rise when the labor market is tight and unemployment low and to fall when the market is loose. With a tight market, employers are compelled by economic necessity to accept workers who, for reasons of race or skill, were previously rejected. People, including a large number of black men, who had not obtained good jobs or any job at all, become valuable employees.

In addition to the overall economic situation other factors were at work in the sixties to improve the nonwhite economic situation: equal employment opportunity laws made discrimination more costly to employers; pressures from the black community induced changes in the status quo in some firms and industries; greater concern for social programs on the part of employers, unions, and governments led to additional training and employment opportunities. Finally increases in income per capita probably induced persons to "buy" relatively more equality and less discrimination. These factors operate to create permanent rather than cyclical advances in the position of discriminated minorities.

It is difficult to determine the relative importance of the various factors

[8]See Claire C. Hodge, "The Negro Job Situation; Has it Improved?" *Monthly Labor Review* (January, 1969).

[9]Note that the figure reports wages and salaries received from work and excludes welfare and related payments. Thus, the changes shown reflect changes in the labor market, not in social welfare policy.

[10]See R. B. Freeman, *Black Elite: Discrimination and Education* (New York: McGraw-Hill, forthcoming).

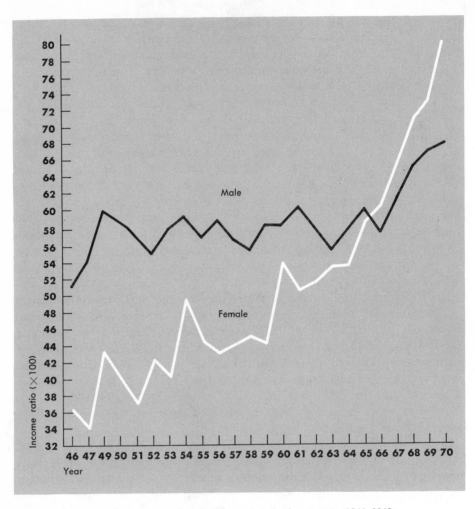

FIG. 5–6 Ratio of black to white median wage and salary income, 1946–1969.

in the advances of the 1960's. For black women the improvements in economic position are probably due to permanent factors and will be long lasting. Additional advances for them require more education and training and advances for women in general. For young college nonwhite men, the test of whether new hiring policies will produce a substantial permanent advance hinges on whether they will be promoted in the future to top jobs that have been historically reserved for whites. The outcome may not be known for many years. For other black men, the fact that the economic recession of the early 1970's did not drop relative incomes to previous levels suggests a permanent advance.

THE LABOR MARKET, INCOME DISTRIBUTION, AND POVERTY

For the vast majority of persons wages and salaries are the principal sources of income and the key determinant of their standard of living. As a result of labor-market and other economic forces, some individuals obtain great wealth whereas others are exceedingly poor. We examine next several aspects of the way in which the United States economy distributes income among persons: the extent of income inequality; the labor-market status and the living conditions of the poor; public programs to alleviate poverty.

The Distribution of Incomes

The extent to which income is equally or unequally distributed in a society is a major determinant of social well-being. Critics of market economies, ranging from Karl Marx to political reformers, often cite inequality of incomes as a major flaw of capitalism. According to Marx, the low income of workers relative to capitalists is one of the forces leading to social revolution. Conservatives and some businessmen, on the other hand, worry about the need for large monetary incentives, and inequality of incomes, to induce persons to undertake risky entrepreneurial ventures. How is income distributed in the United States? How much of the national product goes to the very rich? How much to the very poor? Why are some persons more likely to be poor than others?

Table 5–5 shows the distribution of income among families in post-World-War II America. At the top of the distribution are the wealthy—the 5 percent of families who receive 15 percent of total income. At this level income from stocks, bonds, and other property is important. More than two-thirds of all dividend payments and half of property income accrues to persons in the upper income brackets. In 1969 when the mean income of *all* families in the United States was $10,500, the mean income of the top 5 percent was more than $31,000.

At the other end of the spectrum are the poor—the 20 percent of American families who receive just 5.4 percent of aggregate income. For these persons, property income is virtually nonexistent; they depend on earnings in the labor market and/or on public assistance. By modern standards, their income and living conditions are grossly inadequate. According to the federal government's definition of poverty—which in 1971 was an income of $3,800 or less per year for a nonfarm family of four[11]—most of these families live in dire poverty.

[11]To get a notion of the "adequacy" of an income of $3,800 for a family of four, note that this income amounts to $2.60 per person per day for all living expenses: food, housing, clothing, and so on.

Table 5–5   DISTRIBUTION OF MONEY INCOME, MEAN INCOME, AND SHARE OF AGGREGATE RECEIVED BY EACH FIFTH AND TOP 5 PERCENT OF FAMILIES AND UNRELATED INDIVIDUALS, SELECTED YEARS, 1947–1969

Year and Income	Mean Income before Tax (current Dollars)	Percentage Distribution of Aggregate Income					
		Lowest Fifth	Second Fifth	Middle Fifth	Fourth Fifth	Highest Fifth	Top 5 Percent
Money Income							
Families							
1947	3,566	5.1	11.8	16.7	23.2	43.3	17.5
1957	5,483	5.0	12.6	18.1	23.7	40.5	15.8
1962	6,811	5.1	12.0	17.3	23.8	41.7	16.3
1966	8,423	5.4	12.3	17.7	23.7	41.0	15.3
1969	10,500	—	—	—	—	—	—

Source: Ida S. Merriam, "Welfare and its Measurement," Eleanor B. Sheldon and Wilbert E. Moore. eds., *Indicators of Social Change* (New York: Russell Sage Foundation, 1968), p. 735.

Their members constituted a large fraction of the more than 20 million poor Americans in 1971. Many families in the second fifth of the income distribution are also poor or just above the poverty line.

Poverty and the Labor Market

Although poverty or near-poverty occurs among all types of people, the poor have certain distinctive characteristics:

Two-fifths are children under 18
One-fifth are over age 65
One-third are nonwhite
One-half live in the South
One-quarter are in families headed by women

The reasons for poverty are complex, involving economic, social, and cultural forces. Simply in terms of income distribution, three factors contribute to low incomes: the absence of substantial property or capital earnings among the poor; low wages or salaries in the labor market; and relatively low public assistance.

The position of the poor in the labor market deserves special attention. First, it must be noted that very few are poor because they are unwilling to work. Only the aged, who are not expected to work and who may be unable to do so because of health or compulsory retirement rules, are generally out of the labor force. Nearly three-quarters of the 4.5 million non-aged heads of poor families worked for some time in 1966. Of the 1.2 million heads of non-aged households who did not work, a third were ill or disabled, half were women with young children, and many others attended school or could not find work.

In families with working heads, *irregularity of work*—spells of unemployment or employment in part-time positions—contributes to the poverty of about 4 in 10 families. The remaining families were poor despite the fact that their heads worked full-time through most of the year. Here poverty is attributable to low wages. The male head of a family of four working 40 hours a week, 52 weeks a year, at the minimum wage of $1.60 per hour earns just $3,328 during the year—$472 below the poverty line.

The principal reason for the low wages of these men is a lack of education and skill. According to a recent study of income distribution by Jacob Mincer of Columbia University, approximately two-thirds of differences in the wages and salaries among men are due to differences in years of schooling and in work experience.[12] At the bottom of the income distribution are those with few years of schooling and little fruitful experience. Of course, these two factors are not independent of one another, for individuals who lack schooling get few opportunities for the job training or experience that leads to high-paying positions.

The Life of the Poor

The effect of poverty on living conditions is best described by the poor themselves:

> Maybe if I have four potatoes I will fry them and give them all to go around. Sometimes we don't eat. When the check comes I don't have maybe $3 left. With those $3 we have to eat. Sometimes we eat and sometimes we look at each other.

> The only place we can refer for charity hospitalization is the University Medical Center in Little Rock (150 miles away). But even then, they are so crowded that the doctors always have to make prior appointments and make sure space is available.

> The house is in bad condition and every time it rains the water comes in. I've called public housing many times and they just tell you over the phone, "What am I to do about this?" And the roof leaks, and the water comes through the windows. This is a health hazard. My children get sore throats and they are sick all the time.

> [My daughter asked] "Why is all them doctors out in the hallway?" I said, "Doctors?" She said, "Yeah, they all got needles in their hands." . . . There's junkies, dope addicts, and the rats—don't mention them. They are going hungry now because I ain't got no food.[13]

[12]Fiftieth Annual Report, *National Bureau of Economic Research*, p. 63.

[13]All of these statements are from witnesses before the President's Commission on Income Maintenance Programs, as quoted in the Commission report *Poverty Amidst Plenty: The American Paradox.*

The final question of concern is obvious: How can the poverty of families with heads unable to work because of age, illness, or responsibility for children, or of families with heads working intermittently or at low pay be alleviated?

Most economists, public officials, and poor persons were dissatisfied with the programs of the 1960s. The existing system of income assistance, although it aids many, leaves 13 percent below the poverty line. Unemployment compensation is limited in size and coverage. In some states, the Aid to Families with Dependent Children programs encourages the breakup of poor families by requiring the absence of fathers. Social Security and other social insurance plans exclude or pay particularly low benefits to persons likely to be especially poor.

Several new programs have been proposed. Many persons favor a "negative income tax" or income supplement scheme by which dollars will be paid directly to persons with very low incomes. According to the President's Commission in Income Maintenance Programs, "Enactment of a universal income supplement automatically would reproduce part of existing cash assistance programs, and eliminate or reduce many of the inequities, inadequacies, and inefficiencies in Public Assistance and other programs. The Nixon Administration Family Assistance Plan of 1971 is one form of a negative income tax, aiding the working poor as well as those unable to work.

The main difficulty with negative income taxes is their effect on the incentive to work, especially on persons with limited earnings capacity. To take an extreme case, assume that the government specified $3,000 per year as the national minimum income and paid persons with lower income the difference between their income and $3,000. The persons who expected to earn less than $3,000 would have no monetary incentive to work and those who earned a bit more relatively little incentive. The 'working poor' who made $4,000 a year would lose all of the subsidy and increase their income by just $1,000 over the guaranteed minimum.

To maintain the incentive for work and reward the 'working poor' the Commission's program, like other negative income tax schemes, offers *graduated* payments to the poor. A family of four with no income, for example, would receive the guaranteed minimum income. If the family earns $1,000, the government would reduce the income supplement by less than $1,000 say, to $2,500. In this way persons who work are not penalized by a compensating loss of income assistance. Even so, however, the income offered by the $1,000 job is reduced considerably.

How serious is the threat to work incentives? Several experiments with graduated negative income taxes have been sponsored by the U. S. Government to estimate the impact of negative taxes on labor supply. In these experiments a limited number of families are provided with income supplements and their behavior studied. While all of the evidence is not in, it appears that negative income taxes of the type being considered "do not induce immediate and widespread withdrawals from the labor force."[14]

Another set of programs that can be used to aid the poor concentrates on increasing the wages of those with low earning capacity. There are two principal ways of increasing wages: by legislation of stronger minimum wage laws or by provision of additional training for poor persons.

It is obvious that minimum wage laws, which require all persons in covered industries to receive the legal minimum, can raise the pay of some workers. By extending coverage of the law and increasing the minimum allowable wage, the income of some will be increased. However, with higher wages employers will find it advantageous to hire fewer persons with limited skills. For those remaining fully employed the law is a boon; for those who lose regular employment, it is a bane. Most economists do not believe that substantial increases in minimum wages by legislation are a sensible way to raise the income of the working poor.

The alternative to minimum wages is to provide additional manpower training and development. Programs such as the Manpower Development and Training Act, for example, may add to the job skills and earning power of trainees. Other programs such as the Neighborhood Youth Corps and Work Incentive Program, may provide useful work experience to persons who have difficulty obtaining first jobs or part-time work. Some suggest that the federal government serves as an "employer of last resort," hiring and training poor persons who cannot find appropriate jobs.

Finally, to help poor persons who want to limit the size of their families, family planning programs can be expanded to provide information and services. In this way each American family will be able to decide voluntarily on its appropriate size.

[14]H. W. Watts, "The Graduated Work Incentive Experiments: Current Progress" *American Economic Review* (May 1971) p. 16.

Selected Readings

Burgess, Leonard R., *Wage and Salary Administration in a Dynamic Economy*. New York: Harcourt, Brace & Jovanovich, 1968.

Douty, H. M., *Nineteenth Century Wage Trends*, BLS Staff Paper No. 2. Washington, D.C.: U.S. Department of Labor, 1970.

Freeman, R. B., *Black Elite: Discrimination and Education*. New York: McGraw-Hill, forthcoming.

Galenson, Walter, *A Primer on Employment and Wages*, 2nd ed. New York: Random House, 1970.

Hicks, J. R., *Theory of Wages*, 2nd ed. New York: St. Martin's, 1963, Chaps. 1, 2.

Livernash, E. Robert, "Wages and Benefits," in *A Review of Industrial Relations Research*, Vol. I. Madison, Wisc.: Industrial Relations Research Association, 1970, pp. 79–144.

Reddaway, W. B., "Wage Flexibility and the Distribution of Labor," in B. J. McCormick and E. Owen Smith, eds., *The Labor Market*. Baltimore: Penguin, 1970.

Rees, Albert, *The Economics of Trade Unions*. Chicago: University of Chicago Press, 1962.

Rules of the Work Place,
Collective Bargaining,
and Legal Enactment

Every industrializing society, as Chapter One explained, creates arrangements to define and to administer a vast complex of rules applicable to work places and to relations among managers, workers and their organizations, and government agencies. This network of rules consists of three elements: procedures for establishing regulations, the substantive rules themselves, and the procedures for settling disputes over their application to particular situations.

The following are examples from the millions of rules in American industrial relations.

It is agreed that a total of twelve (12) minutes per day is a fair and reasonable time for the changing of clothes before and after work which is to be paid to each employee in the bargaining units at each plant, and that such time is to be considered as work time for all purposes under this Master Agreement. . . .

(Swift and Company and Amalgamated Meat Cutters and Butcher Workmen)

The right and power to select and hire all employees, to suspend, discipline, demote or discharge them for reasonable cause, to promote them to supervisory or other positions, to assign, supervise and direct all working forces to maintain discipline and efficiency among them, and to exercise the other customary functions of the management for carrying on of the business and operations, are recognized as vested exclusively in the Company. Such right and power shall not be exercised arbitrarily or unfairly as to any employee and shall not be exercised so as to violate any provision of this contract.

(Consolidated Edison Company and Utility Workers Union)

In all cases of promotion, . . . and in all cases of increase or decrease of forces, the following factors shall be considered. However, only where both factors 2 and 3 are relatively equal shall continuous service be the determining factor.

1. Continuous service (seniority)
2. Ability to perform work
3. Physical fitness

(United States Steel Corporation and United Steelworkers of America)

Foremen shall not select or designate a substitute. The regular or substitute shall be the person to select his own substitute, and shall in no way be responsible for the work performed by the same, but no foreman shall be compelled to accept a substitute who is incompetent or otherwise incapacitated, and if the regular's or substitute's selection should fail to appear on time or should be incapacitated, the foreman shall direct that another substitute shall be secured. . . .

(Typographical Union No. 6, New York, and Newspaper Publishers)

Hourly employees are terminated when they reach the age of 70.

(TVA and Tennessee Valley Trades and Labor Council)

No driver shall allow anyone, other than employees of the Employer, who are on duty, to ride on his truck except by written authorization of the Employer, except in cases of emergency arising out of disabled commercial equipment or an Act of God. This shall not prohibit drivers from picking up other drivers, helpers or others in wrecked or broken down motor equipment and transporting them to the first available point of communication, repair, lodging or available medical attention. Nor shall this prohibit the transportation of other drivers from the driver's own company at a delivery point or terminal to a restaurant for meals.

(Teamsters, National Master Freight Agreement and Southeastern Area Over-the-Road Agreement)

Each employee of the executive branch of the Federal Government has the right, freely and without fear of penalty or reprisal, to form, join, and assist a labor organization or to refrain from any such activity, and each employee shall be protected in the exercise of this right. . . .

A labor organization shall not call or engage in a strike, work stoppage, or slowdown; picket an agency in a labor–management dispute; or condone any such activity by failing to take affirmative action to prevent or stop it. . . .

(Executive Order 11491, October 29, 1969)

No employer having employees subject to any provisions of this section shall discriminate, within any establishment in which such employees are employed, between employees on the basis of sex by paying wages to employees in such establishment at a rate less than the rate at which he pays wages to employees of the opposite sex in such establishment for equal work on jobs the performance of which requires equal skill, effort, and responsibility, and which are performed under similar working conditions, except where such payment is made pursuant to (i) a seniority system; (ii) a merit system; (iii) a system which measures earnings by quantity or quality of production; or (iv) a differential based on any other factor other than sex. . . ."

(Public Law 88–38, June 10, 1963)

Rules such as those cited above are set in many ways: by the regulations and policies of management; by the decrees, decisions, or orders of government agencies and the courts; by labor organizations on issues such as dues and initiation fees; by the interpretations of arbitrators of collective bargaining agreements; and by the customs and traditions which become established in every continuing work place. In the United States collective bargaining is a major form of rule setting.

COLLECTIVE BARGAINING[1]

"Collective bargaining" refers to three separate forms of labor-management activity: negotiations over the terms of a new or reopened agreement, administration of an existing agreement, and consultation on matters of common concern to the parties. These processes are not always readily separable in practice.

Negotiations

The process of negotiating a new agreement varies widely from one union–management relationship to another. In a number of industries smaller firms often follow the pattern set by a larger competitor or by an association, simply making minor adjustments in the pattern-setting agreement to take account of special conditions. In larger firms—and particularly in leading negotiations—bargaining is a more complex process.

The process of agreement making customarily proceeds through a series of stages. At the outset, the union presents a long and extravagant list of demands. In many instances, the management responds by submitting its own long list, which typically leaves the parties very far apart. Although this exchange may seem a ritual, it serves many purposes. By putting forward many large demands, the parties disguise their real positions and provide room for maneuver as bargaining proceeds. They explore a wide range of problems which have been of concern to each. They satisfy their constituents or principals by seeming to back numerous proposals, only to scale down many demands or abandon them later in the negotiations. They uncover and recognize problems which have been previously avoided. A proposal may be advanced and explored, only to be put aside for more serious negotiations in a future year.

After the initial presentations, a period of probing follows during which each side tries to clarify the proposals of the other and marshal arguments and facts against them. As bargaining moves along, each side may begin to formulate a combination of proposals or a "package" which it considers a possible basis for settlement. The packages offered give the other side a clearer sense of the priorities attached to various items and concessions to be gained.

[1] This section is adapted in part from Derek C. Bok and John T. Dunlop, *Labor and the American Community* (New York: Simon & Schuster, 1970), Chap. 7.

Items excluded from a package may be expected to be dropped from the final settlement.

Eventually, with or without mediation, before or after a work stoppage, an agreement will be reached. It is a "package settlement" in the sense of a resolution, in one way or another, of all issues in dispute for a period. The meeting of minds typically is arrived at first during informal talk between key negotiators, and later the proposed settlement is presented for acceptance by the full negotiating committee on each side. The tentative agreement is then reduced to contract language, often with the advice of lawyers and after much further discussion over details or wording.

After the agreement has been reached between the negotiators, ordinarily it must be approved by the principals. On the union side ratification may be required by the membership, by a specified group of elected delegates, or by an elected wage policy committee as in basic steel. Management negotiators may need the approval of the president or the board of directors in a company or the membership or directors of an association.

Collective bargaining over the terms of an agreement can be better understood if it is recognized as *three-way* negotiations. There are "negotiations" between the union leaders and their constituents and also between the management representatives and their principals. The negotiations across a collective bargaining table tend to mask these other two "negotiations," but they are vital in establishing the priorities of each side. A labor organization is composed of members with conflicting as well as common interests. The skilled and the unskilled, the pieceworkers and the dayworkers, the young and the older workers and those in various departments or work places under the same agreement do not have the same preferences. A choice has to be made among the needs and interests of these diverse groups. Various company officials also may have different views about negotiations even in a single company. There can be no settlement in collective bargaining until there are in effect three settlements, one within the union, one within management, and one across the table.

The bargaining process is also influenced by broad economic forces. Workers, union leaders, and managers are constrained by the forces of supply and demand in the market. If a union pushes wages up much above the market equilibrium, many members will lose their jobs because the amount of labor demanded depends on wages. Employers may try to hire nonunion labor or, more likely, nonunion employers will expand in the market since they enjoy a cost advantage. In the 1920's expansion by nonunion concerns and replacement of union workers in the coal industry wrecked the United Mine Workers; organization dropped from a majority to a small minority of miners in the space of a few years. Employers also face market constraints. If they offer very low wages, few persons will be willing to work for them. If they pay excessively high wages their costs will exceed those of competitors and they will be driven out of business.

Bargaining Disputes

When management and workers are unable to reach an agreement, they may resort to strikes or lockouts. The strike and lockouts are to be understood as means of stimulating a change in position and inducing the parties to reach an agreement. Economic conflict, or its threat, may cause a management to improve its offer or a union to reduce its demands. The prospect of a test of strength forces each side to reassess its position by weighing its goals and priorities against the costs of conflict. After workers have walked the picket line and management has had its operations shut down both sides may change their position on disputed issues.[2]

The power of a strike or lockout to compel agreement varies with economic conditions. When the market is tight, strikes are very costly to employers whereas workers may be able to obtain outside work easily. For this and other reasons strikes generally vary with the business cycle, rising when unemployment is low and falling when it is high. It is often asserted that strikes or lockouts are unprofitable. "What a waste, to strike for a 10-cent-an-hour increase when you lose three weeks of pay at $200 per week. It would take over 150 weeks or three years to make up for the lost pay." Statements like this are misleading, for they ignore the possibility of obtaining work during the strike period or of otherwise using the available time for useful activity: fixing up the house or resting.

Administration of Collective Bargaining Agreements

In American industrial relations a contrast is to be drawn between the periodic *negotiation* of an agreement and the day-to-day process of *administering* the agreement and applying its provisions to specific situations. This distinction is not made in some other industrial relations systems. In the British system, for example, the parties negotiate over all questions that arise without limitation of the duration of the agreement and without restriction on the resort to strike or lockout. The American view envisages a specified duration of the negotiated contract between the parties and a method, typically a grievance procedure including arbitration, to administer and resolve disputes during the term of the agreement.

The process of administering a collective bargaining agreement provides the flesh and blood to the bare bones of the contract language. The provisions of the agreement may have been written under very great time pressure late at night and the full implications not fully agreed upon by the negotiators or

---

[2] In economic conflict damage may be inflicted on third parties in addition to those directly involved. Inconvenience and costs may be borne by the public. The Taft–Hartley Act and the Railway Labor Act provide procedures, in cases affecting the national interest or the nation's health and safety for government intervention, beyond mediation, to delay the stoppage for a limited period. But a final settlement cannot be imposed save by special legislation as has been done several times in the past decade in the railroad industry.

their committees. New circumstances may arise that were envisaged in the negotiations or conflicts may be discovered among different sections of the agreement which need to be resolved. The negotiators may have been unable to resolve all differences over the application of a provision and may have deliberately chosen to leave ambiguities to be resolved on a day-to-day basis. The administration of the agreement creates precedents which the parties tend to follow in similar circumstances, at least until the issues may be reviewed in negotiation.

The core of the day-to-day administration of agreements is a well-administered grievance and arbitration procedure. Such procedures provide for several stages at which a grievance may be considered, beginning with the individual employee and his superior and often ending with an outside arbitrator. Grievance procedures provide an important measure of 'due process' at the work place, guaranteeing workers an opportunity to overturn unfair and illegitimate managerial decisions. As one report stated:

> A major achievement of collective bargaining, perhaps its most important contribution to the American work place, is the creation of a system of industrial jurisprudence, a system under which employer and employee rights are set forth in contractual form and disputes over the meaning of the contract are settled through a grievance procedure. . . . The gains from this system are especially noteworthy because of their effect on the recognition and dignity of the individual worker. This system helps prevent arbitrary action on questions of discipline, layoff, promotion, and transfer, and sets up orderly procedures for the handling of grievances. Wildcat strikes and other disorderly means of protest have been curtailed and effective work discipline generally established.[3]

A further indication of the effectiveness of grievance procedures is the fact that managements in a number of companies or plants without union representation have installed such procedures, even including resort to outside arbitration in certain cases such as discipline or discharge.

Joint Consultation

In a number of labor–management relationships the top representatives of both sides meet during the term of the agreement, apart from negotiations over the terms of an expiring agreement, to discuss general common problems or specific issues. In some instances neutrals may assist the parties. These *joint study committees*, as they are often called, are designed to gather facts, to define more precisely problems which need attention, and to propose solutions to be reviewed more formally by the contract negotiators at a later date. The parties may wish to improve morale, reduce the volume of grievances, improve

[3]*The Public Interest in National Labor Policy* (New York: Committee for Economic Development, 1961), p. 32.

productivity; or make a systematic review of the wage rate structure, seniority districts, a complex adjustment to major technological changes, an incentive plan; or they may choose to study the pension and retirement area.

The time required to gather the facts or study these complex problems is much longer than that available in the 60 days typically devoted to negotiations before the expiration of an existing agreement. Moreover, the more relaxed atmosphere during the life of the contract may provide a more constructive setting in which to explore tough issues. These joint committees afford the leaders of both sides an opportunity to exchange ideas and compare developments apart from the tension of contract negotiations with the prospect of a strike or lockout to induce agreement. These committees may also help to set a constructive setting and spirit for upcoming contract negotiations.[4]

LEGISLATIVE ENACTMENT AND ADMINISTRATIVE ORDERS

In addition to the independent actions of managements and the role of collective bargaining in organized work places, many substantive rules of the work place are established by legislation or by decisions of government agencies. Although the scope of collective bargaining is more extensive in the United States than in other countries, the role of government in rule setting at the federal, state, and local level has been growing. Often these government regulations are influenced by the conflict, and occasionally the agreement, of labor and management organizations in the political and legislative arenas.

From its inception in this country the labor movement has sought to secure certain legislation which it regarded as favorable. Indeed, legislation affecting the work place might be described as setting the rules by governmental decision rather than by resort to direct collective bargaining. At the first meeting of the American Federation of Labor in 1881[5] it adopted a platform providing for the prohibition of child labor before age 14, uniform apprenticeship laws, restriction on sale of products made from prison labor, prohibition of attaching wages of workers for debts, abolition of conspiracy laws as applied to labor organizations, and other legislation. The famous Bill of Grievances, a program of legislation of the AFL, presented to Congress in 1906, urged the enactment of an adequate eight-hour-day law, exclusion of Chinese labor, a law forbidding the towing of more than one undermanned and underequipped vessel, and the like. Safety legislation, with administrative enforcement, was an important objective for many years of the mine, maritime and railroad unions.

With the advent of the New Deal in 1933 the range of government inter-

---

[4]For a discussion of the work of some of these committees, see James J. Healy, ed., *Creative Collective Bargaining* (Englewood Cliffs, N.J.: Prentice-Hall, 1965).

[5]The Federation was then called the Federation of Organized Trades and Labor Unions of the United States and Canada.

vention in rule making expanded a great deal. The Wagner Act of 1935 and the Taft-Hartley law of 1947 prescribe the procedures for establishing collective bargaining relationships, define unfair labor practices by managements and unions, and specify limits to collective bargaining as in the prohibition against the closed shop and the requirement that plant guards be in separate bargaining units. The Landrum–Griffin Act of 1959 regulates the internal affairs of unions including union elections and a bill of rights for union members. These various rules are elaborated and interpreted by administrative agencies and the courts.

A vast body of social legislation has been enacted in the past generation prescribing rules of the work place. These include wage and hour legislation, Social Security, and unemployment compensation. Title VII of the Civil Rights Act was designed to eliminate discrimination in employment on account of race, color, religion, sex, or national origin. Other legislation in some states is concerned with discrimination on account of age. Very complex questions concerning the meaning of these legislative enactments, in the great variety of industrial conditions, preoccupy various administrative agencies and the courts, labor and management organizations, civil rights groups, other voluntary associations, and government agencies seeking to interpret and apply the legislative statutes.

A major issue confronting the society concerns the relative roles of collective bargaining and legal enactment in setting the rules of the work place. In some countries such as France, for example, paid vacations and holidays are the subject of social legislation whereas in the United States they are left entirely to collective bargaining or management discretion under the constraints of the labor market. The collective bargaining method probably results in much greater diversity because bargaining power differs and because managements and workers in different industries and localities have different preferences among forms of compensation. Collective bargaining permits greater decentralization in initiatives for change. Legislative enactment represents a much deeper penetration of government into the private sector, often with the burdens of heavy bureaucracy, inflexibility, uniformity, and inefficiency.

The question also arises as to how much the results of collective bargaining developed by private parties may be modified on account of considerations of public interest. The legislation against the closed shop or a court order finding a particular seniority system to be discriminatory on account of sex or race constitutes a considered interference with free, private collective bargaining. It is not clear how effective legislation or administrative rulings can be against the combined interests or agreement of the parties to collective bargaining. In many cases legislation may, over a period of years, induce changes in ideas, beliefs, and values as well as in contract language, while in other cases the parties may well find means to circumvent the announced public policy. The question of the appropriate limits of collective bargaining and legislative enactment is posed sharply in times of inflation when compensation settlements exceed "guideposts" or the wage standards of an income policy. The reconciliation of the results of collective bargaining and objectives of public policy is a continuing theme of rule setting at the work place.

MAJOR CATEGORIES OF RULES

Among the thousands of rules that are applicable to any modern work place, at least three large categories exist in all instances: rules relating to compensation, to the operation of the internal labor market, and to procedures used to resolve grievances and disputes over the application of the rules. The substance of these rules, of course, varies from one industry to another, but rules of these types are found everywhere.

Rules Relating to Compensation

The *method of wage or salary payment* is one of the most significant compensation rules. Employees may be paid by a time method, such as by the hour, day, week, month, or year; they may be compensated by some measure of output, such as per piece, per ton, per mile, or by a commission on sales, or under complex plans in which a number of separate factors influence the payout. The amount of take-home to workers and the extent of labor costs per unit of output to management are significantly dependent on how the method of compensation is administered.

A pilot of a commercial airline, for instance, is paid in part at an hourly rate for each flight hour that varies with the speed of the aircraft and depends upon whether the flight hour is accrued during the day or the night, in part by the mileage flown during the month, and in part by the gross weight of the aircraft flown, and in addition compensation is influenced by a highly technical body of rules providing various guarantees and special payments for various contingencies such as for training, deadheading, or standby status[6] Sewing machine operators in the garment industry are paid by the piece, and the rate per piece may vary with the price line of the finished garment. Coal miners at the mine face in the past were paid a tonnage rate per ton of coal mined with these rates varying with the breadth, thickness, and other qualities of the coal seam and the working conditions. With the mechanization of both the cutting and the transport operations in underground coal mines, day rates have tended to replace tonnage rates. Under all incentive pay schemes workers and their organizations have a particularly keen interest in the quality of materials, the maintenance of equipment, the quality of supervisory organization,

[6]For a discussion, see John M. Baitsell, *Airline Industrial Relations, Pilots and Flight Engineers* (Boston: Harvard University, Graduate School of Business Administration, Division of Research, 1966), pp. 57–110.

and other factors which influence earnings with given piece or incentive rates.

The sharp distinction between hourly pay for production workers and monthly salaries for white-collar employees and executives has been eroded in a number of companies in recent years with all employees, after an initial period, being placed on salary. These developments make labor costs more of a fixed cost with respect to short-run changes in output. The stabilization in employment may compel adjustments to fluctuations in demand that take the form of greater variations in inventory and the shifting of work operations from one plant location to another.

The method of wage payment is not an accidental or capricious decision, but is closely related to the technology and competition of the industry. Thus, there have been shifts away from piecework or incentive methods of pay in both the Soviet Union and the United States. Modern automated machinery and continuous process industry, as in oil refining and chemicals, are better suited to day-rate pay schemes. Rapid technical change requires frequent revisions in piece rates or incentive schemes with attendant conflict, withholding of effort, and gamemanship between industrial engineers and workers over the rates.

Another large complex of compensation rules relates to *fringe benefits*, the phrase commonly used to refer to paid vacations and holidays, health and welfare plans, insurance, pensions, sick leaves, and a variety of other benefits to workers, their families, and dependents or to retired employees. These elements of compensation have expanded very rapidly since World War II (see Table 6–1) and in many industries now constitute 20 to 30 percent of labor costs. Thus, in appraising earnings or costs per hour it is essential to recognize that in most enterprises a further "add on" is involved in such benefits.

The distribution of fringe benefits often involves social considerations such as length of service in the plant, size of family, age, illness or other afflictions. Certain individuals receive high fringe benefits under the established rules on the basis of need rather than on the basis of contribution to output. It is not surprising that in negotiations conflicts should arise among groups of workers in reaching decisions on the size and distribution of these benefits. There are many competing uses for the money available from management for increases. A major function of labor organizations is to develop an internal consensus in negotiations on these divisive questions.

The rules defining these benefit plans tend to be rather complex and as a consequence both management and labor organizations have attracted professionals working in such areas as pensions, medical care, and insurance. Even a relatively simple benefit such as paid vacations, which was almost unknown for manual workers 30 years ago and is now almost universal under union agreements, involves complex rules. The rules must determine who is eligible, for what length of vacation, for what pay, how preference is to be awarded among workers as to the time of year they take their vacations, and

Table 6–1   JOB EVALUATION

Factor	Bulk Palletizer Attendant Selecting Dept.	Production Crewheader Decorating Dept.	Shift General Foreman Corrugating Dept.
Skill			
1. Pre-employment Training	.5	.5	1.0
2. Employment training and experience	.5	2.0	3.0
3. Mental skill	.5	1.5	2.5
4. Manual skill	.5	—	—
Responsibility			
5. For materials	.5	1.7	3.0
6. For tools and equipment	.2	.2	.1
7. For operations	.5	2.5	3.5
8. For safety of others	1.0	.5	.5
Effort			
9. Mental effort	.4	.8	1.2
10. Physical effort	.5	—	—
Job Conditions			
11. Surroundings	—	—	—
12. Hazards	.4	—	—
Total	5.5	9.7	14.8
Rate Group	6	10	15
Wage Rate per Hour Effective March 1, 1970	$2.645	$2.97	$3.53

what is to happen when a worker wishes to take his vacation at a different time of the year than suits the management. To these general questions may be added many more details such as whether employees should be allowed or required to work through vacation periods for additional money, or whether voluntary severance of employment, a discharge, or death during the year should entitle an employee, or heirs in the case of death, to partial payment of vacation benefits. The establishment and administration of the rules of the work place must involve these and many other related issues.

The *wage scale*, or the wage rate assigned to each job classification, is pivotal to managements and workers alike. In many industries collective bargaining was initially concerned primarily with the wage scale and traditional working conditions governed other issues. In craft-type negotiations the setting of the rate for the journeyman and the schedule of apprentice rates historically exhausted the bargaining process. But in industrial, office, or other work places with a large number of tasks, job classifications, or occupations, the setting of wage rates involves complex issues of the relative wages of employees engaged in interrelated work in the same or contiguous departments. Morale and productivity and costs are significantly affected by relative rates, and a considerable amount of time in many negotiations, and in the grievance procedure, is taken up with the claims of occupations, groups, or individuals who believe they are underpaid compared to others and who contend their jobs have been improperly described and classified in the wage structure.

Although wage rates for hundreds of jobs could be bargained for a single plant, in recent years formal job evaluation plans have become very common in industry. *Job evaluation* is a procedure designed to rank jobs on a formal basis and to measure the worth of a job for compensation purposes in relationship to other jobs. The formal plan may be a product of collective bargaining, as in the basic steel industry, or have been instituted by management with the union having bargained to challenge the valuation of any job, as in the glass-bottle industry.

A job evaluation plan requires written detailed description of work operations encompassed by each job. The descriptions provide a bench mark to determine at a later date the extent to which jobs have changed as a result of technological or organizational changes, and are used to rank jobs according to such factors as skill, responsibility, effort, and job conditions. These general factors are often further divided into specific factors and a weight assigned to the relative importance of each. Each job is then reviewed to assign an evaluation for each factor and a total evaluation for the job. These evaluations of particular jobs are then grouped into labor grades to correspond with pay brackets.

An illustration from the Owens-Illinois Hourly Job Rating plan may help to convey the procedures of job evaluation. This plan has twelve factors shown in Table 6–1. The point evaluation is presented for each factor for three jobs in three different departments. The total points for a job determines its labor grade which in turn specifies the wage rate under the collective bargaining agreement. (The blanks shown for some factors mean that the job is rated at base or minimum norm for that factor.) The points assigned to each factor constitute a measure of the relative contents of these jobs.

Job evaluation should not be regarded as a black art or a formula approach to wage setting; rather, it is a tool for estimating the appropriate wage for *specialized jobs* within a firm given market-determined wages for more general jobs. The jobs in table 6–1, for example, are so specific that few if any employees in the general labor market identify themselves as working in them. Persons obtain these positions by promotion, transfer, or bumping in the internal labor market rather than by hiring from outside the firm.

Those who set wages for various job classifications in a plant or office cannot ignore the rates in other work places for comparable work. Comparisons between inside rates and the outside market are particularly significant for job classifications, such as janitors, maintenance crafts, and certain clerical jobs which are common across industries and where there is direct hiring from outside. But even in these instances the actual content of the jobs, the working conditions, stability of employment, opportunities for promotion, quality of supervision, and other factors affecting the desirability of jobs are not reflected in a simple comparison of job titles and wage rates.

Rules Relating to Internal Labor Markets

A large part of the complex of rules of a work place concern the relative rights of individual employees in particular jobs. These "property rights" in a job are defined in terms of contingencies which occur in the work community. Who shall be laid off when work is slack? When employees are to be rehired following a temporary shutdown, in what order shall they be returned to work? When vacancies arise, shall they be filled by promotion from within or by hiring from outside? If vacancies are filled by promotion, which employees shall be considered and which shall be promoted? These questions are not only vital to the individual employees whose lives are immediately affected, but they affect the costs and efficiency of management and the influence of the union as an organization.

The rules relating to different types of movements within a single work community depend upon the work environments. Thus, in many industrial plants where employment tends to be relatively steady, labor organizations are likely to pay special attention to rules relating to layoffs, promotions, transfers, and retirements, but to be relatively unconcerned with hiring, leaving that to management discretion. On the other hand, in construction or in longshoring, where employment on individual jobs is of short duration, labor organizations are particularly concerned to establish rules affecting hiring and transfers, leaving management considerable discretion with layoffs or discharges.

The principle of *seniority* has received wide acceptance in determining the job rights of workers. Seniority is normally defined as *length of continuous service*. In prescribing layoffs, transfers, or promotions most rules specify that relative ability or the ability to meet the basic requirements of the job must be considered, before or after a trial period. (See the rule in the basic steel industry quoted on page 100. The relative weight to be given to seniority as compared to other factors is typically the subject of detailed and complex rules and is interpreted through decisions by management, supplemental agreements, or arbitration.

There are a number of reasons for the extensive use of seniority. It is an objective measure as compared to such other criteria as ability, physical fitness, and skill, and tends to minimize the extent of personal favoritism in selecting employees for movement. Both unions and management commonly recognize that the investment of years of service creates an "equity" in a job which should afford an employee greater protection and consideration. **111**

Experience is an important indicator of investments in on-the-job training and the ability to meet contingencies that arise. Many unorganized companies observe the principle of seniority as closely as companies which are parties to collective bargaining agreements. However, seniority may be strongly opposed by civil rights groups and others who regard the principle as hindering the advancement of those subject to previous discrimination.

There are often serious questions over the applicability of seniority. The unit or job territory in which seniority is exercised may be a point of conflict. Years of continuous service in a department or on a particular machine need not be the same as seniority in the plant as a whole. One employee may have superior departmental seniority and another longer plant service. The weight accorded to plant and departmental or unit seniority need not necessarily be the same for temporary layoffs as compared to promotions. A narrow seniority district is likely to mean that the next several men in line for the job have experience with the operation and can fill the position with relatively little training. On the other hand, with wide seniority units the next senior man may have little experience in the appropriate department or operation and may require considerable training which may be expensive in productive and capital utilization.

Rules Relating to Grievance Procedures and Arbitration

Almost all collective bargaining agreements provide for grievance procedure that specifies a series of steps to be taken by the parties in the resolution of disputes during the life of the agreement. Most grievances originate with individual employees who are union members, although the union is required under rulings of the courts to represent fairly, without hostile discrimination, all employees in the handling of grievances whether or not they are union members or pay periodic dues and assessments to the union. Typically, an employee will first present a complaint orally or in writing to his foreman or supervisor, with or without the assistance of the union steward or representative. Most grievances are settled at this stage. If an accomodation cannot be reached the agreement ordinarily provides for several levels of possible appeal to progressively higher echelons within the union and management hierarchy. If still no settlement is achieved, an outside neutral arbitrator may be requested by the dissatisfied party to make a final and binding decision. In the United States, in contrast to most countries, such arbitration is conducted by private arbitrators paid for jointly by the parties.[7] The use of arbitration is usually tied to an agreement not to strike or lock out over arbitrable issues. The master agreement between Swift and Company and the Butchers provides for the following steps:

[7]An exception is the railroad industry, where boards of adjustment established by the Railway Labor Act perform the arbitration function.

Union	Management
1. The aggrieved employee (with or without union representative) or the union representative	1. The foreman or forelady of the department
2. Union representative	2. General foreman or divisional superintendent
3. Plant grievance committee and local union representative	3. Plant superintendent
4. International union representative	4. General superintendent of the company

If the grievance is unresolved after these steps it may be submitted to an arbitrator "whose decision shall be final and binding on the parties. In making said decision, the arbitrator shall be bound and governed by the provisions of this contract and restricted to its application to the facts presented to him involved in the grievance."

Not all issues in dispute can end up in the arbitrators lap even if this leads to official work stoppages during the life of the contract. For example, in the major automobile contracts, disputes over production standards used in the measured daywork system are not subject to arbitration; the UAW and the auto companies believe that better settlements may be mutually achieved by permitting work stoppages under carefully controlled circumstances after the national leaders on both sides have sought to resolve the dispute. There have been relatively few such stoppages. Most agreements limit arbitration narrowly to the "interpretation and application" of the agreement. The following provision from the basic steel agreement is typical:

> The Board of Arbitration shall have jurisdiction and authority only to interpret, apply, or determine compliance with the provisions of this agreement and such local working conditions as may hereafter be in effect in the plants of the Company, insofar as shall be necessary to the determination of grievances appealed to the Board. The Board shall not have jurisdiction or authority to add to, detract from, or alter in any way the provisions of this agreement.

The procedures for arbitrating grievances developed earliest in the printing, shoe, apparel, and coal industries, and had their origin in the desire of parties to resolve disputes over the terms of agreements by voluntary arbitration. In 1930 no more than 8 to 10 percent of all collective bargaining agreements provided for arbitration as the final step in the grievance procedure. The expansion of unionism into mass production industries in the 1930's, and particularly the influence of the National War Labor Board during World War II, led to a rapid growth in grievance arbitration. By 1949, 83 percent of agreements contained such provisions, and currently more than 95 percent include arbitration clauses for at least some categories of grievances.

113

With the decisions of the Supreme Court in 1960 in three steelworker cases, popularly known as the *Trilogy*, the power and the prestige of the arbitration process in the United States became fully established. The court stated in part:

> In the absence of any express provision excluding a particular grievance from arbitration, we think only the most forceful evidence of a purpose to exclude the claim from arbitration can prevail. . . . Since any attempt by a court to infer such a purpose necessarily comprehends the merits, the court should view with suspicion an attempt to persuade it to become entangled in the construction of the substantive provisions of the labor agreement, even through the back door of interpreting the arbitration clause, when the alternative is to utilize the services of the arbitrator.[8]

The arbitrator is empowered to interpret the agreement, including the question of the arbitrability of the grievance under the agreement, and to create appropriate remedies.

The parties themselves have the opportunity to shape the arbitration process in the course of negotiating a collective bargaining agreement. They can define the types of grievances subject to and not subject to the jurisdiction of the arbitrator. They can designate which subjects are precluded from strike during the agreement term and which may be subject to strike. They can provide for a continuing umpire to handle all cases, for special arbitrators to handle complex cases such as those relating to job evaluation or wage incentives, or for a series of *ad hoc* arbitrators. They may provide, as many agreements do, that the arbitrator shall be selected in a particular case by the Federal Mediation and Conciliation Service or by the American Arbitration Association.

The formal grievance and arbitration procedures established in an agreement may also be shaped decisively by the various levels of the labor and management organizations in day-to-day operations. The procedures may be used informally for consultation in advance of problems or legalistically to fight cases. The parties may approach grievances only to win them as in combat or may prefer to settle disputes in practical terms. Some grievance and arbitration procedures are clogged with cases and others have only a small volume after the initial step. Some procedures require months or even years to handle cases whereas others resolve all disputes in a matter of days or weeks. The relationship of the parties is nowhere more clearly revealed than in the operation of the grievance procedure, and the quality of these relations may be expected to have a significant impact on periodic contract negotiations.

The grievance procedure is used by both union organizations and managements as a means by which information is channeled between the top and the bottom of these hierarchies.[9] The top-management officers and the union leaders

[8]United State of America v. Warrior and Gulf Navigation Company, 363 U.S. 574, (1960), pp. 584–85.

[9]See John T. Dunlop and James J. Healy, *Collective Bargaining: Principles and Cases* (Homewood, Ill.: Richard D. Irwin, 1953), pp. 78–81.

114

who follow carefully the status of grievances are able to keep in touch with developments of concern to individual workers. New problems and interests are often rapidly reflected in grievances. As a channel of information, the grievance procedure is likely to be more reliable than most other chains of command since both union and management representatives are aware that the grievance may go to a higher step including an outside arbitrator. Any statement will be subject to check by the other side before a superior officer or arbitrator. The grievance procedure is less subject to self-serving statements than are most chains of command within an organization.

The grievances presented may often be a symptom of other questions than the issue formally raised. The real problem may be a foreman or a steward in a department. Grievances may reflect an internal political struggle within a union or a conflict between the production, industrial relations or industrial engineering departments in a management. Subordinates may not be receiving proper instructions. The grievance is often indicative of some deeper maladjustment, and the experienced representative of the union and management will seek out the real and submerged difficulties.

SUMMARY

The rules of the work place in the United States are established by management in unorganized work places or through collective bargaining where organized representation exists. In addition, legal enactment determines a number of rules. Collective bargaining encompasses a variety of activities: the negotiation of the terms of agreements, the administration of agreements through the grievance procedure and arbitration, and joint consultation during the period of an agreement.

It provides a means for workers to participate in decisions affecting their livelihood.

The setting up of rules at the work place and the application and administration of those rules may receive relatively little public attention, except when accompanied by a work stoppage, but these daily accomodations are vital to workers, labor organizations, and managements; the routine handling of these problems is essential to an industrial society.

Selected Readings

Bernstein, Irving, *Turbulent Years, A History of the American Worker, 1933–1944*. Boston: Houghton Mifflin, 1970.

Bok, Derek C., and Dunlop, John T., *Labor and the American Community*. New York: Simon & Schuster, 1970.

Dunlop, John T., *Industrial Relations Systems*. New York: Holt, Rinehart & Winston, 1958.

Taft, Philip, *Organized Labor in American History*. New York: Harper & Row, 1964

Ulman, Lloyd, "American Trade Unionism—Past and Present," in Seymour E. Harris, ed., *American Economic History*. New York: McGraw-Hill, 1961

American and Foreign Industrial

Relations Systems

Countries differ widely in the way they handle labor problems. Wages, left largely to labor and management in the United States, are the subject of government arbitration tribunals in Australia. Grievances over management decisions at the work place are reviewed by workers' councils elected by employees in Yugoslavia, by private arbitration under collective bargaining agreements in the United States, and by a variety of government bodies in France. For purposes of comparison and contract, this chapter identifies the main features of the American industrial relations system and gives a broad picture of the labor scene in three other countries, the U.S.S.R., Japan, and Yugoslavia. International comparisons help show what is distinctive about our arrangements and illuminates discussion of alternative modes of organizing the work process.

COLLECTIVE ORGANIZATION

A fundamental feature of every industrial relations system is the extent and nature of the collective organization of workers and employers. The main form of worker organization in the United States is the labor union, which represents groups of workers in negotiations with employers and in political and legislative activity. Approximately 28 percent of all nonagricultural employees are union members, affiliated with one of more than 70,000 local unions, which are in turn mainly affiliates of 190 national or international unions. Most of these national unions and more than three-quarters of the entire union

117

membership are members of the AFL–CIO; the remainder are unions which have withdrawn from the Federation as a result of differences in policy or leadership conflicts, as in the case of the Auto Workers or Teamsters, or which have been independent from their formation.

Union membership is substantially concentrated in certain industries— transportation, communications, utilities, construction, and manufacturing—and is relatively infrequent in retail and wholesale trade, finance, services, agriculture, and government employment (Fig. 7–1). More than half the blue-collar work force outside of agriculture is unionized compared to no more than 10 percent of all white-collar workers. Throughout the 1960's the principal

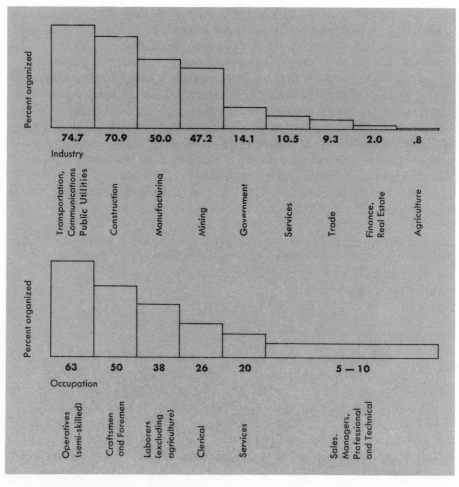

FIG. 7–1   Characteristics of union membership.

area of expansion of the union movement was among public employees. By 1970 nearly 3 million of 14.5 million government workers had joined collective organizations to negotiate over conditions of employment.

The extent of unionization is much smaller in the United States than in most Western European countries (Table 7–1). There are several reasons for this low level of organization. Historically, American employers have opposed unions more strongly than employers in Europe save for France and Italy. More important, American workers lack the class solidarity often found in Europe. Perhaps because opportunities for advancement and geographic movement have been greater in the United States and wages and living standards high and rising, an ethic of greater individualism distinguishes American workers from their counterparts in other countries. An additional factor is the limited organization of government employees in the United States. In many European countries, including France, Austria and Sweden, and in Australia and Japan, government workers are strongly unionized and account for a sizeable fraction of the labor movement.

Many white-collar and public workers in the United States are members of "professional associations"—the American Nurses Association, player associations in professional sports, the American Association of University Professors—that on occasion act in ways similar to conventional labor unions. Police

Table 7–1 UNION MEMBERSHIP AS PERCENTAGE OF NONAGRICULTURAL EMPLOYMENT IN THE UNITED STATES AND WESTERN EUROPE*

	Union Membership (thousands)	Total Number Employed (thousands)	Percentage of Organization
Austria	1,540	2,247	68.5
Sweden	2,165	3,302	65.6
Belgium	1,700	3,407	49.9
Italy	6,320	14,242	44.4
Austrialia	1,475	3,448	42.8
England	8,757	22,621	38.7
Netherlands	1,430	3,978	35.9
Germany	7,996	23,733	33.7
France	3,071	10,243	29.0
United States	17,299	60,770	28.5

*Australian data is for 1963; data relating to other countries refers to 1965.

Sources: U.S. Department of Labor, Bureau of Labor Statistics, Directory of National and International Labor Unions in the U.S., 1967, Bulletin No. 1596 (1968), p. 56; Directory of Labor Organizations: Europe, May 1965, pp. xii–xiii; Directory of Labor Organizations: Asia and Australia (March, 1963), pp. x–xi; and International Labour Office, Yearbook of Labour Statistics (1967), Table 3, pp. 276–295.

officers' associations, for example, appear to be the principal cause of the "blue plague," an exotic illness known only to members seeking improved benefits; members of the National Education Association, an organization of a million schoolteachers and administrators, negotiates with school boards in many localities and has resorted to strikes and other collective sanctions to achieve their goals.

Collective organization of business firms in associations or federations for purposes of bargaining is less common in the United States than in other Western countries. Although some employers negotiate together, particularly in local markets such as local trucking, construction, garment, and service industries, most managements bargain separately. National bargaining in railroads and certain basic steel companies is the exception.

SPECIAL CHARACTERISTICS OF COLLECTIVE BARGAINING IN THE UNITED STATES

Within the organized sector of the economy, labor–management negotiations occur in a framework of law, custom, institutional structure, and economic forces that vary from country to country. Collective bargaining in the United States is distinguished by five relatively unique features.

1. *Decentralization.* Industrial relations is decentralized in the United States, with great power and activity at the level of local unions. American workers are covered by more than 150,000 *separate* union–management agreements, most of which relate to employees in a single plant or firm or metropolitan area. In Europe and Australia, on the other hand, union agreements are negotiated for large numbers of employers working for many different firms. Collective bargaining in Sweden, for example, consists initially of national negotiations between the central federation of labor unions and the central management association, followed by special industry and plant negotiations. In Great Britain, industry-wide bargaining prevails; in France, regional bargaining—in both cases followed by plant negotiations.

Since agreements in the United States relate to specific plants, they take direct account of local work practices and market conditions. As a result the bargained wage is the actual wage paid by companies. Under more centralized systems, where wages are determined in the first instance by broad national, industrial, or regional bargaining, the bargained wage is often supplemented by managers or local negotiators to reflect local conditions. In periods of great demand for labor, this has resulted in "wage drift," with actual wages increasing more rapidly than the bargained national increase.

2. *Exclusive representation.* Employees in a plant or other bargaining

unit choose a single union to represent them in the American industrial relations system. They express their preferences—for union *A* or union *B* or no union—in elections supervised by the National Labor Relations Board and abide by majority vote. The practice of exclusive representation is partly the result of the American political custom of electing single representatives by majority vote and partly the result of trade union fears of "dual unionism" (rival unionism) weakening the labor movement. In countries where workers have been historically divided along political or religious grounds—in Belgium, France, Netherlands—a different system of representation is found, with rival unions representing different groups of workers at the same work place and in the same occupations. In France, in particular, Communist, Socialist, and Catholic unions often coexist in the same establishment, each representing its own members and bargaining with management through a precarious common front.

3. *Detailed contracts.* Because negotiations in the United States are exceptionally oriented toward specific issues at the work place and toward the wages and conditions of employment in individual plants, collective agreements are more detailed than in other countries. A typical contract in the United States may be 100–150 pages long, regulating the many work rules—promotion criteria, grievance procedures and the like—described in Chapter 7. Most European contracts are, in contrast, limited documents which cover little more than a minimum scale of wages, some benefits, and standards of working conditions. The specific problems of individual plants are resolved outside of the master labor contract.

4. *Industrial conflict and union ideology.* The position of the labor movement in the American capitalist economy is in some ways peculiar. On one hand, the degree of industrial conflict in the United States exceeds that in most countries. Early American labor history is replete with instances of industrial violence—the Homestead strike (1892 steel), the Battle of the Running Bulls (1937 autos)—and of numerous and lengthy nonviolent conflicts in the form of strikes and lockouts. Though declining over time, the fraction of man-days of work lost due to strikes and lockouts is higher in the United States than in most other advanced countries.

On the other hand, American unions support the main economic and political institutions of the society. No stronger statements in favor of private enterprise come from other segments of the community than from many labor leaders. The ideology of the labor movement is "business unionism," which may be viewed as radical in wage demands but conservative with regard to the economic institutions of private enterprise.

The coupling of a high incidence of conflict and business unionism reflects many features of the American environment, including the decentralized bargaining which focuses attention on narrow economic gains, a history of interunion rivalry, relatively high and increasing wages, and the individualism of workers and managers.

5. *The role of government.* Government's role in the American industrial system is distinctive in two respects. It is difficult to find a country with such extensive and detailed regulation of the bargaining process and of the internal procedures of unions. The law in the United States establishes an electoral procedure for determining union representation. If a group of workers or a union wishes to organize a plant, they request an election supervised by the National Labor Relations Board. The Board determines the extent of the election district—whether it includes all workers in a plant, unskilled workers only, or workers in several localities—and regulates the election process. The election of union officials and their handling of pension funds and other union moneys is also the subject of national law. Under the Landrum–Griffin Act of 1959 unions must hold elections periodically and file reports of their finances with the Labor Department annually.

The government also plays a part in determining the subject of bargaining, prescribing some topics that must be bargained about and forbidding bargaining over others, including the demand for a closed shop.[1] Under the National Labor Relations Act, union and management are obligated to bargain in good faith over "rates of pay, wages, hours of employment, and other conditions of employment." The National Labor Relations Board and the courts interpret this law to make topics such as bonuses, pensions, and provisions for checkoff of union dues, mandatory topics for bargaining. Within the broad scope of the law, however, the issues actually considered for bargaining vary depending on the problems particular to firms or industries.

Extensive and detailed regulation of the bargaining process and internal union democracy is accompanied, oddly enough, by a relative absence of government suggestion, recommendation, or prescription of the substantive results of bargaining. With the brief exception of the wage guideposts in the period 1962–66 and an occasional call for noninflationary wage increases, the United States government leaves the substance of bargaining to labor and management. It requires companies and unions to bargain but does not seriously pressure them except through voluntary mediation to reach any particular agreement or, with rare exceptions in national emergencies, to reach an agreement at all. Although legal interpretation has changed since the Wagner Act was passed in 1935, the spirit of the United States law can still be represented by the statement of one of the Act's original sponsors, Senator Walsh of Massachusetts: "When employees have chosen their organization, when they have selected

[1] A closed shop, illegal since the Taft–Hartley Act of 1947, makes union membership a prerequisite for a job with the employer involved.

their representatives, all the bill proposes to do is to escort them to the door or the employer and say, 'Here they are, the legal representatives of your employees.' What happens behind those doors is not inquired into, and the bill does not seek to inquire into it."[2]

The combination of regulation of procedural details and substantial laissez-faire in collective bargaining is strange in comparison with other countries. It is, however, consistent with a highly decentralized industrial relations system, in which collective bargaining reaches into the details of business operations, including almost every aspect of working conditions. Since the issues under consideration are so very detailed and involve the economic behavior, interest, and expertise of specific managements and groups of workers, their resolution is viewed as best determined by the parties involved. The law seeks to contain the conflicts which arise in bargaining by regulating the bargaining process and determining permissible modes of conflict.

Development of the American Labor Movement

Although many features of American collective bargaining became important in the 1930's with the passage of the New Deal legislation, the earlier development of the labor movement significantly influenced present institutions and practices. The predominance of a business union ideology is traceable to the ability of the unions of the American Federation of Labor, founded in 1881, to develop viable national organizations in the 1860's, 1880's, and 1890's in contrast to the failure of the more utopian Knights of Labor. The Knights, an organization containing genuine trade unions and many socially concerned persons, was oriented toward legislation and producer cooperation rather than collective bargaining and narrow economic goals. Its diffuse structure and diverse membership did not provide cohesive economic strength to survive setbacks. The Knights sought to encompass all who worked for a living, all members of the producing class in a single organization.[3] Concern with dual unionism and the desire for exclusive representation dates from the struggle of the AFL with the Knights for membership.

The political orientation of the labor movement also has its origins at the turn of the century. With most government officials passively, if not actively, opposed to unions, the AFL opted for "voluntarism," in which labor and management would settle disputes without government intervention. According to AFL President Samuel Gompers, the trade unions were to shun a labor party and "reward their friends and punish their enemies" regardless of party affiliation.

[2]*79 Congressional Record 7660* (1935).

[3]Bankers, lawyers, doctors, and those who sold liquor or made their living by its sale were excluded from membership.

The period between the end of World War I and the depths of the Great Depression saw a retrenchment of the union movement. Membership fell from 16 to 9 percent of the nonagricultural work force. Employment declined in the strongly organized industries of coal mining, railroads, and construction (after 1926). The unions were unable to organize the new, expanding mass-production industries such as automobiles, rubber, and electrical manufacturing. Employer opposition and a loose labor market after 1929 made organization most difficult.

The coming of the New Deal heralded a major change in the legal framework of industrial relations. The passage of the Norris–LaGuardia law (1932) restricted the role of courts to issue injunctions in labor–management disputes, and outlawed the yellow-dog contract under which companies made the rejection of union membership a condition for employment. By restricting the courts' use of injunctions, the law freed unions to strike, picket, and engage in other collective acts in disputes with management without legal interference.

In contrast to the Norris–LaGuardia Act, which took the courts out of labor–management relations, succeeding legislation has increased the government role. The Wagner Act provided federal government protection of the right of employees to organize and join unions. The government policies compelled a change in the harsh opposition of many employers to labor unions and precluded coercive practices against union members and leaders. In providing for government-conducted elections, administered by the National Labor Relations Board, to determine the preferences of employees for union representation, these policies changed the methods of organizing from the picket-line and small-group persuasion to political-type campaigns and electioneering. These procedures also resulted in looser ties of many members to their unions since employees were called upon only to indicate their preference through the ballot. The government determination of election districts, including the choice between craft and industrial groups, constituted a degree of government intrusion into internal union affairs that was not widely perceived in 1935.

As the economy began to recover from the Depression, union membership expanded. Many workers reacted to the sufferings of the Depression and the favorable political atmosphere by joining collective organizations. In the 1930–1940 decade, union membership increased from 3.2 to 7 million persons. Under government protection unskilled and semiskilled factory workers in the mass-production industries of automobiles and steel were organized into viable trade unions and employer counteroffensives resisted. Competition between the AFL and the Congress of Industrial Organizations, a group of AFL secessionists interested in organizing workers along industrial lines and led by John L. Lewis, seemed to spur rather than deter unionization. The gains from this period of intense organization were solidified during the period of tight labor markets, wartime controls, and dispute settlement procedures associated with World

War II. The tripartite War Labor Board helped spread grievance procedures with arbitration and the acceptance of union security clauses in contracts; it provided a setting in which the new collective bargaining relationships were developed, often under the supervision of national leaders of labor, management, and the public.

The role of government in industrial relations was altered with the Taft–Hartley Act of 1947 which placed greater restrictions on union activity. For example, unions were forbidden to engage in secondary boycotts, jurisdictional disputes were outlawed, the closed shop was prohibited, and procedures were instituted to deal with labor disputes which threatened the nation's health or safety. States were allowed to establish "right-to-work" laws placing limitations on the application of union security provisions in collective bargaining agreements. In part, this change in government attitude from encouraging unionism to restricting union powers was a result of the success of the union movement and specifically of an epidemic of strikes in 1946, when automobile, coal, steel and other workers struck for higher wages.

The Landrum–Griffin Act of 1959, passed in response to a series of sensational hearings on labor racketeering and other abuses before Senator McClelland's committee, further regulated union activities. Regular elections of officers and disclosure of union finances were required to assure internal union democracy and financial responsibility. Despite fears and hopes that these laws would weaken union power, their effect on the labor movement appears to have been relatively slight. They have, however, contributed to the greater independence of rank-and-file members and the tendency to reject agreements negotiated by officers in periods of high employment.

In the 1950's and 1960's union membership grew at approximately the same pace as total nonagricultural employment, prospering in the principal areas which were organized during New Deal days but expanding very slowly in the South and into industries such as agriculture or services which were previously unorganized.[4] Only in the public sector was the frontier of organization significantly extended. Secondary-school teachers, municipal, county, and state employees, policemen, and firemen, began joining unions or transforming their traditional associations into de facto unions n the late 1960's. Unionization of public employees creates new problems in industrial relations—whether such workers should have the right to strike, and how governments will negotiate wages when tax rates and budgets are fixed at periodic intervals by legislative bodies. These issues will be at the forefront of the labor scene in years to come.

[4]The AFL merged with the CIO in 1955 and a second "federation" (American Labor Alliance) was organized in 1969 by the Teamsters and the Automobile Workers, both previously affiliated with the AFL–CIO.

FOREIGN INDUSTRIAL RELATIONS SYSTEMS

If decentralization is the keystone of American industrial relations, centralization characterizes labor relations in the Soviet Union. Wage rates are set by the government, managers are largely limited in their employment decisions by directives from state planners, and labor unions are run from above by government officials. On the other hand, individual workers are free to select and change jobs so that the allocation of labor to different industries, occupations, and regions is influenced by wages and salaries. The way in which wages are determined is critical to the functioning of the Soviet economy.

Ostensibly, wages are set by the government to increase output and productivity and to obtain labor in desired jobs. Two principles guide government wage-setting:

1. The use of substantial occupational, industrial, and regional differentials to motivate workers to upgrade skills and seek employment in appropriate enterprises. Differentials between jobs are determined by a national job-evaluation plan in which jobs are given a numerical rank or grade according to the difficulty of work, skill required, and related factors. Jobs that obtain a high evaluation are paid a premium over jobs rated low in the spectrum. Carpentry, for example, is rated higher in the evaluations than common labor and thus receives higher pay. Additional premiums are added to draw workers into particular industries—for instance, steel or aerospace—or to compensate for regional disadvantages, as in Siberia.

2. The extensive use of *piece-rate* or incentive methods of wage payment to motivate workers to perform well on the job. Under piece-rate wage systems, a "norm" is set for a job on the basis of units produced or some related criterion. Workers who exceed the norm receive substantial financial rewards whereas those failing to fulfill norms are penalized. The Soviets believe that piece rates motivate individuals to work especially hard and increase output and productivity.

Even in the Soviet system, however, wage decrees do not completely solve the problem of wage determination. Wage decisions made by planners or government bureaucrats must be translated into actual wages at the work place. In the translation process, managers, individual workers, and unions can influence wages. With a piece-rate system, for example, each enterprise has some leeway in deciding (1) the jobs in the plant corresponding to the

[5]See Emily Clark Brown, *Soviet Trade Unions and Labor Relations* (Cambridge, Mass.: Harvard University Press, 1966); Walter Galenson, "Wage Structure and Administration in Soviet Industry," in J.L. Meij, *Internal Wage-Structure* (Amsterdam: North-Holland Publishing Company, 1963), pp. 300–334.

jobs in government regulations, (2) the norm for the job in the plant and (3) the job assigned to different workers. Manipulation of these variables can circumvent nationally determined wage standards. Norms can be loosened or tightened, they may or may not be changed with technological advances and changes in materials, workers may be officially placed in jobs with skill requirements and wages differing from those of their actual job, and so on.

In the years immediately preceding the wage reform of 1956, inappropriate norms and job assignments appear to have had a substantial influence on wages. From 1947 to 1956 the Soviet government did not decree any wage increase but average wages went up by 27 percent. In the machine tool industry, norms were typically overfulfilled by 100 percent; throughout the economy unskilled workers "disappeared," with virtually no one placed in the two lowest job categories. Unplanned factors—market forces, perhaps individual or group "bargaining" with managers at the work place—created this enormous discrepancy between planned and actual wages—an experience analogous to that of Western Europe when "wage drift" caused a divergence between bargained and actual wages. Since 1956 the Soviet government has attempted to keep its wage system more in line with economic realities and has experimented with a degree of greater decentralization.

Measured by the proportion of workers in unions, the Soviet Union is the best organized country in the world. Approximately 94 percent of the work force are union members. In the early years of Soviet communism the unions were a relatively independent force whose leaders argued for increased worker benefits and gradual industrialization in economic debates. During the purges of the 1930's however, independent leaders were "eliminated" by Stalin and the unions lost independent influence on Soviet policy. They became a tool used by government to motivate workers and control their behavior. With Stalin's death, some greater role was assigned to the unions, though their basic policies continue to be set by the union officials in obedience to government and party decisions.

Trade unions perform three functions in the Soviet system. First, they administer a variety of social insurance programs, including pensions and disability insurance, that are in the province of the Social Security Administration in the United States. They also provide low-cost vacation programs, recreational and educational opportunities, and access to housing built by the enterprise. By placing these benefits under union auspices, the Soviet government guarantees nearly complete organization of workers.

A second function of Soviet unions is the protection of individual workers from illegal or unfair managerial decisions at the work place. In theory, unions safeguard worker rights by assuring managerial compliance with labor regulations, processing grievances over the interpretation of work rules such as job transfers or the right to fringe benefits, and by helping determine the job norms.

127

In practice, lack of independent power and great stress on fulfilling output plans by the Communist Party has limited union effectiveness in these areas. It is not uncommon to find local unions criticized in the Soviet press for failing to protect workers.

The third job of labor unions is to serve as a "school of communism," indoctrinating workers with communist ideology and pressing them to fulfill or overfulfill work norms. Unions help organize "socialist competitions" between factories and provide publicity and awards for workers who overfulfill their norms. When the goal of motivating work has conflicted with the protection of worker rights, Soviet unions have tended to stress the former, probably because their power is derived from above rather than from the workers.

Japanese Industrial Relations[6]

Perhaps the most significant characteristic of Japanese work relations is the existence of "permanent workers" in the modern sector of the economy. These are workers, including union leaders, who are hired by large firms and given extensive technical training in company schools with the expectation that they will work for that particular enterprise for their entire life. Under this system a high school or college graduate who obtains a job with Mitsubashe will normally work for Mitsubashe until he retires at the age of 55.

The lifetime commitment between workers and firms gives the Japanese labor market a distinct flavor. It fosters the organization of unions by enterprise rather than by craft or industry. Under "enterprise unionism," unions are primarily concerned with the specific company in which they are located and have only loose ties to unions in other companies. Often the union is led by white-collar employees, who are more unionized in Japan than in the United States, and negotiates with managers who were former union members. Because of the symbiotic relation between an enterprise union and management, strikes are less likely than in other industrial relations systems. A strike against a single company can injure its competitive position and the long-term economic welfare of its workers.

Most enterprise unions are affiliated with national unions and one of three national federations. Although these broader organizations have no role in local economic issues, they are an important part of the Japanese labor scene. The national unions are the backbone of the socialist parties that represent the "left" in Japanese elections and attempt to set the climate of bargaining by an annual spring campaign—a national demonstration for increases in benefits. The dominant federations differ greatly in their ideology and sometimes compete for workers in the same enterprise.

[6]See Solomon B. Levine, *Industrial Relations in Postwar Japan* (Urbana, Ill.: University of Illinois Press, 1958); Hisashi Kawade, "The Government Industrial Relations and Economic Development in Japan" in Arthur M. Ross, ed., *Industrial Relations and Economic Development* (London: Macmillan, 1966), pp. 66–89.

In addition to permanent employees in large enterprises, the Japanese labor force contains many "temporary workers" in large firms, who are hired with no guarantee of employment, and many employees of similar status in smaller enterprises. These workers are relatively disadvantaged in the market; employers view them as a safety-valve for adjusting the number of jobs in line with business cycles and they are rarely organized by unions. Because they obtain only a limited amount of training in the job, their earnings increase only moderately with age, exclusive of general increases in the wage level. In contrast, permanent employees enjoy substantial wage increases during their lifetimes as a result of continuous upgrading of their skills and the premium placed on seniority for key workers.

For many years, permanent workers in large firms enjoyed a great wage advantage over other Japanese workers. In 1954, for example, firms with 1000 or more employees paid premiums ranging from 25 percent to 100 percent compared to firms with 10 to 29 employees (Table 7–2). Under pressures of a tight labor market and a booming economy, however, the traditional pattern has altered in recent years. To compete for labor, small firms are obligated to offer especially high wages to young workers (Table 7–2, figures for 1964).

The current system of union-management relations in Japan differs considerably from the system envisaged by General MacArthur during the American occupation. MacArthur attempted to set up an American style industrial relations system with "business unionism" similar to that of the AFL and the CIO. A wide variety of economic, historical, and political factors ranging from the disorganization and economic insecurity of defeated Japan to a long tradition of paternalism and deference to leadership doomed his effort. It is not an easy task to transfer institutions developed in one country under a particular set of circumstances to other situations.

Table 7–2 WAGE DIFFERENTIALS AMONG MALE PRODUCTION WORKERS IN JAPAN, BY SIZE OF FIRM AND AGE, 1954 AND 1964

(Average for firms with 10–29 employees or more = 100) Age of Worker and Size of Firm	1954	1964
18		
1000 or more employees	127.0	86.0
10–29 employees	100.0	100.0
20–24		
1000 or more employees	141.0	93.0
10–29 employees	100.0	100.0
40–49		
1000 or more employees	197.0	152.0
10–29 employees	100.0	100.0
50–59		
1000 or more employees	204.0	172.0
10–29 employees	100.0	100.0

Source: Japan, Ministry of Labor, "Basic Survey of Wage Structure."

129

In the years immediately following World War II the Yugoslavia Communist regime adopted a centralized economic system similar to that of the Soviet Union. The plan of 1947 was a 5000-page document with detailed instructions for factories in Serbia and stores in Macedonia. Centralized planning, however, was not well suited to Yugoslavia. In 1950 it was abandoned and Yugoslavia embarked on "worker management," an experiment in combining socialism with decentralized market decision making. The result is a unique industrial relations system in which workers participate, at least nominally, in the affairs of the enterprise to a greater extent than elsewhere in the world.

There are three basic elements to Yugoslav workers management:

1. Worker control of enterprises. As in other socialist countries, the state owns all but the smallest business enterprises in Yugoslavia. Under the Yugoslav constitution, however, the normal managerial authority is legally vested with the workers of the enterprise rather than with government-appointed managers. The workers elect a council which takes responsibility, with the government of the locality, for hiring a "director" to be the chief executive of the enterprise and which participates in decisions regarding output, employment, investment, and the like. (Perhaps because workers hire managers rather than managers hiring workers, the income differential between workers and managers is among the lowest in the world.) The Yugoslavs expect worker participation in managerial decisions to motivate workers and create nonmonetary satisfaction on the job.

2. A market environment. Yugoslav experience with centralized planning in the 1940's convinced them that "the justice of the market is preferable to the justice of subjective administrative allocation." As a result Yugoslav enterprises operate in a market environment, with less direction from above than in other Socialist countries. They compete with one another and with imported commodities for sales to consumers and firms. They compete for investment funds from Yugoslav banks. Prices are, with some exceptions, free to fluctuate in response to market forces.

3. Profit sharing. An intrinsic part of Yugoslav workers' management is the use of enterprise-wide profit sharing to reward workers and motivate efficient production and economic decision-making. When an enterprise prospers in the market and "profits" are high, the income of a worker is also likely to be high, for he receives a share of the profits. When the enterprise does poorly, earnings will be low, possibly falling to the minimum wage guaranteed by the central government. Within limits specified by the government, the workers'

---

[7]See Adolf Sturmthal, *Workers Councils, A Study of Workplace Organization on Both Sides of the Iron Curtain* (Cambridge, Mass.: Harvard University Press, 1964), pp. 86–118; International Labor Office, *Workers' Management in Yugoslavia* (Geneva: 1962), Studies and Reports, New Series, No. 64.

council has the option of dividing part of net receipts between investment in new equipment and "dividends" to workers.

Because workers share in decision making and profits at the level of the enterprise, Yugoslav firms are likely to operate differently from Western firms. On the one hand, there is a danger that workers in highly profitable enterprises will restrict employment and investment so that profits need not be shared among a large number of persons. On the other, the decentralization of firm decision making and the opportunity for worker participation may increase the pleasure derived from work and the intensity of the work effort; it may also facilitate the industrialization and discipline of an agrarian work force in a country without the traditions of a strong management leadership.

Although Yugoslavia relies greatly on the market and on decentralization of decision making, government authorities still exercise considerable control over some aspects of the economy. To assure rapid economic growth, the central government taxes away a considerable fraction of enterprise and personal income for investment purposes. The amount of profits shared among workers is thus limited, and according to Yugoslav opinion polls, less than desired. The allocation of a substantial fraction of national output to investment rather than consumption has, however, enabled Yugoslavia to increase per capita output rapidly and thus to increase consumption in the long run.

The Communist Party also influences enterprises in accord with the goals of the central government. Party members are likely to be especially active in workers' councils and especially sensitive to national plans. On occasion workers have been prevented from increasing their own portion of net income by social pressures and intensive propaganda from party, trade union, and other officials.

A COMPARATIVE VIEW OF THE ORGANIZATION OF WORK

The labor market and industrial relation problems facing various societies are, we have seen, much the same regardless of national and cultural differences. Industrialization and modern technology prescribes many aspects of organizing the work place. Their influence is most direct in determining the occupational structure, training and educational requirements, and wage differentials. The work places of textile mills, oil refineries, and airplane cockpits resemble each other in countries with diverse political and social arrangements as a result of the logic of industrialization.

The comparisons of this chapter also reveal several areas of diversity. Countries can choose between different degrees of centralization and de-centralization; can choose to rely on markets or on governmental decrees; can prescribe the status of labor and management organizations in various ways; can provide individual workers with protection through lifetime employment guarantees,

131

seniority provisions in collective agreements, worker 'ownership' of factories; better functioning markets, social income assistance, and so on. The comparative perspective provides some notion of the range of alternative ways of structuring the workplace and of the potential benefits, costs, and problems of different approaches. Although future technological changes and their consequences for the work force, similarities in consumption behavior, and international exchange of experience may blur some current national differences in the organization of work, differences are likely to persist and may increase in some areas as a result of social choice.

Selected Readings

Alexander, R. J., *Labor Relations in Argentina, Brazil and Chile.* New York: McGraw-Hill, 1961.

Kassalow, Everett M., *Trade Unions and Industrial Relations: An International Comparison.* New York: Random House, 1969.

Milenkovitch, D. D., *Plan and Market in Yugoslav Economic Thought.* New Haven: Yale University Press, 1971.

Sturmthal, Adolf, *White-Collar Trade Unions, Contemporary Developments in Industrialized Societies.* Urbana, III.: University of Illinois Press, 1966.

Taira, K., *Economic Development and the Labor Market in Japan.* New York: Columbia University Press, 1970.

Walker, K. F. *Australian Industrial Relations Systems.* Cambridge, Mass.: Harvard University Press, 1970.

Ward, B., "The Firm in Illyria," *American Economic Review* (Sept., 1958).

133

135